DATE DUE

SMART GROWTH

Ernesto J. Poza

SMART GROWTH

Critical Choices for
Business Continuity
and Prosperity

Jossey-Bass Publishers
San Francisco • London • 1989

SMART GROWTH
Critical Choices for Business Continuity and Prosperity
  by Ernesto J. Poza

Copyright © 1989 by: Jossey-Bass Inc., Publishers
                     350 Sansome Street
                     San Francisco, California 94104
                                &
                     Jossey-Bass Limited
                     28 Banner Street
                     London EC1Y 8QE

Library of Congress Cataloging-in-Publication Data

Poza, Ernesto J., date.
    Smart growth : critical choices for business continuity and
  prosperity / Ernesto J. Poza.—1st ed.
      p.   cm.—(Jossey-Bass management series)
    Bibliography: p.
    Includes index.
    ISBN 1-55542-170-9 (alk. paper)
    1. Close corporations—Management.   I. Title.   II. Series.
  HD62.25.P69   1989
  658'.045—dc20   89-8191
                                                     CIP

Manufactured in the United States of America

The paper in this book meets the guidelines for
permanence and durability of the Committee on
Production Guidelines for Book Longevity of the
Council on Library Resources.

JACKET DESIGN BY WILLI BAUM

FIRST EDITION

Code 8944

The Jossey-Bass Management Series

Consulting Editors
Management of Family-Owned Businesses

Richard Beckhard
Richard Beckhard Associates

Peter Davis
The Wharton School
University of Pennsylvania

Barbara Hollander
The Family Firm Institute

Contents

Preface

Achieving growth and innovation across generations has not been a common discussion topic among entrepreneurs. Nor has it been a simple issue for organizational theorists, researchers, or practitioners to address. Yet the need for study and action is clear; seven out of ten family-owned businesses fail to survive beyond the founding generation (Danco, 1975). Weakened by a slowdown in growth or declining profitability, they fall victim to competitors and either close down or get bought out or merged with more successful businesses. The small percentage of family businesses that do survive past the first generation suffer a perceptible drop-off in innovation and growth (Blotnick, 1984). At this point no one knows precisely how many second-generation family business owners go on to regenerate the business, but I estimate it at less than one in ten.

After twenty-five to thirty years of successful operation, closely held businesses typically find themselves at a crossroads where family life cycle and the cycle of the original product line intersect. In other words, an aggressive new generation is likely to assume leadership from the aging CEO at a time when the original product is in a mature or declining phase in the marketplace. These businesses then face a critical choice: to regenerate or to face organizational decline or even death. It is not my intention to be dramatic. To grow or die seems in fact to be the choice.

The CEO's dilemmas at this critical juncture are many: He wants the next generation to commit itself to the business but does

Note: An increasing number of women are becoming CEOs of closely held businesses. *He* and *she* will be used interchangeably throughout the book.

not want to part with his creation. He wants to support growth opportunities for the next generation but does not want to squander hard-earned assets. He wants successors to enjoy working hard in the family business but prefers to spare them the pain and sacrifice that the founding generation endured.

The successor's dilemmas are equally challenging. Should she work in the family business or launch a professional career with a larger corporation? Should she trust others to protect her ownership interest in the business or ensure control by personally managing the business? Should she work through or ignore lifelong conflicts with her parents or siblings?

The complexity and emotional intensity of these dilemmas make choices at this stage extremely difficult for both generations. In the absence of other mutually attractive options, selling the business for cash frequently becomes the preferred course of action. What was once considered a measure of last resort may come to be seen as the best alternative. This was the case, for example, in the Pabst (brewing) and Bingham (publishing) family businesses. These choices are not easy to make and are therefore tempting to postpone. Postponement, however, invites further decline.

In the evolution of business organizations, two factors make the family business a particularly adaptive system. First, family businesses are by their very nature equipped to respond to the growing need for balance between the achievements of work and the love and spiritual connectedness of family life. And second, macroeconomic changes are pointing toward greater decentralization of production and the growth of smaller-scale enterprises that can be more customer-oriented.

Audience

This book will be useful primarily to three (related) audiences: business owners, their advisers, and scholars of entrepreneurship and family business.

Along with business owners, CEOs, directors, and potential successors in closely held or family-controlled corporations will profit by reading *Smart Growth*. Many owners now acknowledge that business continuity is an important goal but are far from confident of their own ability to revitalize the business across generations. Many board members experience frustration in helping owners stimulate smart growth to ensure survival, family harmony, and prosperity. Most next-generation owners or owners-to-be agonize in a similar fashion over their role in the enterprise and over the complexities of generational transition. This book addresses their concerns from a practical point of view.

Although as a rule consultants to these closely held businesses have a background in one specialized area (for example, accounting, tax law, strategic planning, or family therapy), they are painfully aware of the need to bring a holistic and interdisciplinary perspective to family-owned businesses in search of renewed growth and vitality. Advisers can also be nonfamily professional managers operating as home-office staff, or experts assembled by business owners to serve as a board or team of paid advisers. *Smart Growth* provides new insights, helpful concepts, and implementable approaches to help unblock businesses facing the dilemmas of succession and the crisis of maturing product life cycles.

For the scholarly audience—researchers interested in entrepreneurship, organization development, and family businesses—this book proposes a model of entrepreneurial activity across generations. The methodology it provides for inducing or promoting change in closely controlled organizations will be of interest to business students and executive program participants interested in entrepreneurship and growth.

The purpose of this book is to broaden the range of possibilities for growth and innovation that founders and second- or third-generation CEOs can consider after a productive twenty-five- or thirty-year tenure in their business.

A second purpose of the book is to broaden the repertoire of interventions for bringing about required changes in closely held businesses. Revitalizations such as the ones at Johnson Wax and M. Jacobs and Sons (discussed in Chapters Two and Ten) can often take place only after professional interventions into the systems of ownership, organization, and the family itself have paved the way. Should professional advisers be required, it is appropriate to select them on the basis of their knowledge of these three systems.

My intent in writing *Smart Growth* was to help you, the reader, envision a variety of attractive outcomes from which to choose. The book further provides you with practical action steps for managing the regeneration of the business in accordance with your vision. Examine the ideas contained in this book to judge their applicability to your own business. You know your business best and are therefore the best judge of which growth opportunities will work in your particular circumstances.

Overview of the Contents

Part One contains an introduction to the cycles of growth and decline that businesses face. Chapter One explores the dismal record of entrepreneurial organizations in preserving the spirit present at their inception. Owner life cycles, product cycles, and the crisis brought on by their simultaneous ebb are explored. At this point, CEOs face perhaps the most critical choice in their professional and family lives: to regenerate and grow the business or look on as organizational arteries harden. I discuss early warning signs to watch for so that you can mobilize energy for change in your company while there is still time.

Chapter Two weighs the respective merits of decisions to go public or to sell, maintain, or grow the business. The concept of *interpreneurship,* or entrepreneurial activity across generations, is discussed.

Part Two acquaints the reader with a variety of approaches for managing the stages of business growth and developing a smart growth strategy. In Chapter Three I explore the process of growth—its sprints and pauses—and consider the sources of energy for growth. Activities that you can initiate to increase the energy for growth in your company are presented. Building on these suggestions, I explain how to start the process of growth.

Chapter Four, which details a sequence of growth opportunities, is a kind of brainstorming session on growth options. I discuss the importance of small successes to validate and further new growth opportunities, as well as the importance of saying no to certain growth options in order to grow appropriately.

The need to match external growth opportunities with personal visions and company resources and capabilities is the focus of Chapter Five. The importance of a family mission statement in selecting appropriate growth opportunities is also established in this chapter.

In Chapter Six I set forth a plan for branching out from the core business and building on the company's strengths—my aim being to help you develop a living strategy rather than undertake some grand analytical exercise. I also examine ways in which you can strengthen commitment to your chosen strategy.

Chapter Seven focuses on a key implementation issue— aligning the structure with the growth strategy. A new growth strategy calls for a different organization and financial structure; I propose organization designs and financial structures that are conducive to the success of new ventures. Changes in structure and roles that create learning opportunities for next-generation family members are described, as well as other "soft" organizational changes that complement these structural changes.

Part Three deals with ensuring continued growth in accordance with business and family vision. In Chapter Eight I stress how important clear vision is for leaders of expanding businesses. The major challenge that mature companies face is finding a way to bring people with diverse interests together to work for the good of the organization and the shareholders—the challenge of developing a collective vision of growth.

Chapter Nine expands on the theme introduced in Chapter Six by presenting a commitment-building approach to strategy development, the strategy-setting meeting.

In Chapter Ten I present recent findings on new-venture management and analyze managerial practices that encourage innovation and entrepreneurship across generations. This chapter should make it easier to implement smart growth in the day-to-day management of the business.

In the concluding chapter, Chapter Eleven, I outline the ten essential characteristics of a family business that is ready to grow.

Letters to the CEO and to the next generation translate the book's findings into a personal call for action. Finally, a section on key tactics sums up recommendations for regeneration gleaned from my years of helping businesses choose smart growth. My hope is that this book will help you pursue business growth with confidence.

Acknowledgments

This work is the product of several years of consultation and action research with many different businesses. These companies ranged from third- and fourth-generation family businesses to new ventures and *Fortune* 500 companies. The book could not have been written without access to the CEOs, owners, presidents, and senior managers of these companies. To preserve their privacy, I do not mention most by name; in general, fictitious names have been used instead. But the contributors will recognize ideas they have helped to shape.

Significant contributions to the book were made by Richard Beckhard, my consulting editor, teacher, professional colleague, and long-time friend. Very helpful comments made by James Brogden, Léon Danco, Ivan Lansberg, Edith Perrow, Sharon Rogolsky, Andrew Sharkey III, and John Ward have been incorporated into the text. The early conceptual guidance provided by John Aram, assistant dean of the Weatherhead School of Management, Case Western Reserve University, and the research assistance provided by Michale Murphy, also of Case Western Reserve, were very valuable.

Barbara Bird, John Davis, Peter Davis, Philip Dawson, Barbara Hollander, Donald Jonovic, Charles Kieffer, Murray Low, Perry Pascarella, Karen Saum, and Peter Senge contributed stimulating reflections.

During the preparation of the manuscript, Jesse Epstein acted as my mentor in writing skills and helped make the book more reader-friendly. His friendship throughout this process was a real bonus. Connee Miller was a dedicated and reliable administrative assistant, who remained good-humored through the vicissitudes of computer and printer malfunctions.

Finally, I want to acknowledge Lawrence (Bo) Burr, CEO of a family-owned business, whose idea it was to call this book *Smart Growth.*

Cleveland, Ohio   Ernesto J. Poza
June 1989

To my family, Karen and Kali,
with love, commitment,
and the hope for continuing growth

The Author

Ernesto J. Poza is president and owner of E. J. Poza Associates, a business consulting firm in Cleveland, Ohio, that specializes in promoting business growth, assisting with succession planning, and managing change. Poza holds a B.S. degree (1972) from Yale University in organization and management and an M.B.A. degree (1974) from the Massachusetts Institute of Technology (M.I.T.)'s Alfred P. Sloan School of Management. As a professional consultant, he has acted as an adviser to top managers on strategic management issues, organizational restructuring, regeneration, and transition management.

Among the closely held businesses he has served in the United States and Latin America are Mars, Inc., McCormick, Grupo Alfa (Mexico), Banco de Chile, Master Industries, Grupo Salcedo (Ecuador), and Epstein, Gutzwiller and Partners. He has also consulted for publicly held organizations like General Motors, Allied-Signal, Bethlehem Steel, James River Paper, Goodyear, Atlantic Richfield, Corn Products Corporation, and others.

Poza has lectured to family business groups and at M.I.T.'s Sloan School of Management, Yale University, the University of Michigan, Case Western Reserve's Weatherhead School of Management, and the Escuela de Negocios Adolfo Ibáñez in Chile.

In addition to his consulting activities, Poza conducts seminars and workshops on family business topics for associations in the United States, Canada, and Latin America. His most recent articles include "Managerial Practices to Support Interpreneurship and Continued Growth" (1988), "Improving Morale and Customer Service in Banks: A Case History" (1987), "Comprehensive Change-

Making" (1985), and "Twelve Actions to Strong U.S. Factories"
(1983).

His biography appears in *Who's Who in Finance and Industry* (1987–88) and *Who's Who of Emerging Leaders in America*
(1989). He lives with his wife, Karen, and daughter, Kali, in More-
land Hills, Ohio.

SMART GROWTH

Cycles of Business Growth and Decline

In Part One I discuss the cycles of business growth and decline. In Chapter One I explore how these cycles correlate with the life cycle of the primary product or product line that the business offers. Predictable patterns of birth, fast growth, maturity, and decline/ death or decline/regeneration all occur within a major cycle of approximately twenty years. In family-owned businesses, these cycles occur in conjunction with cycles linked to the developmental phases of the CEO's life and the life cycle of the rest of the owning family (including members of the next generation). Powerful forces in a family business's existence then intersect that may propel the business and the family toward total revitalization or leave it mired in inaction, facing the pain and dissatisfaction that accompany the decline of a firm or a family.

Chapter One also discusses the biggest risk to a business at the crossroads of decline or regeneration: that of becoming paralyzed by competing interests or collective lack of interest. Many families have no clear vision such as the original founder-entrepreneur possessed. They lack clarity about where they want to go and what they want the business to become.

Decline is the option most exercised by family-owned businesses: as mentioned earlier, less than 30 percent survive beyond the first generation. But this is an option that is exercised by default rather than by choice. Only concerted action will make decline the least likely option. And concerted action will seldom take place without a good, compelling reason for regenerating the business. The need for or desirability of growth can stem from a growing family's need for the wealth a growing business can produce, from excitement about unexplored growth opportunities envisioned by the new generation, or from a crisis, a death, or the frustration of dealing with a declining business. Only once the need for growth is crystal clear to all involved can the revitalization horn be sounded and a better path than decline sought.

Chapter Two argues that growth is the best alternative to decline and the eventual death of the business. Other possibilities include selling the business, going public, or entering a maintenance/holding mode to build a stronger foundation for the next stage of growth. There can be good reasons for deciding in favor of each of these—they are also explored in Chapter Two.

Regeneration through interpreneurship—entrepreneurial activity across generations—is generally the most promising way to promote growth but also the most demanding of capital and leadership attention and time. It is therefore the option that demands the most clarity and singleness of purpose—this at a time (in the second generation and beyond) when a team of entrepreneurs and not a single founder will be in charge. Developing a commonly held vision of a desirable future for the firm and the family is the best means of arresting decline and promoting family business growth.

1

Ten Warning Signs of Decline and What to Do About Them

Organizations typically find themselves at a crossroads sometime after twenty-five or thirty years of successful operation. That crossroads is created by the arrival of a new generation in positions of leadership in the business and by the end of the successful run of the original product's cycle. In other words, as the founder or current CEO's life cycle ebbs, the next generation assumes greater responsibility; simultaneously, the product that made the earlier generation's business successful has matured or begun its decline in profitability and perhaps even sales volume. These coincident life and product cycles throw businesses into a turmoil out of which decline is the most likely outcome. Thus the first order of business at the crossroads should be survival.

Decay and divisiveness set in very easily in stable and declining businesses. Centralization forces often increase, emphasizing control, reducing participation, eroding individual responsibility, and inhibiting innovation. Resistance to change then often increases and leads to turf protection and rejection of new and better alternatives. If resources are scarce—or are perceived to be scarce in comparison to the fast-growing years—competition and in-fighting for control spread. As this vicious cycle progresses, both founders and next-generation CEOs are often blamed for the problems of employees or family members. They become the scapegoats. Divisiveness becomes the predominant characteristic of the business

3

and the owning family. Conflicts in the family may reach crisis proportions; and in the business, morale suffers and turnover increases, because of the perception that nobody cares.

According to one recent study, small, private organizations are much more susceptible to these problems than larger, often public institutions (Cameron, Whetten, and Kim, 1987). The momentum of larger and public organizations insulates these from threats to their survival. The larger pool of accumulated resources— both people and money—of these larger, public enterprises acts as an environmental buffer.

This survival threat initially keeps smaller, often private businesses nimble and competitive in the face of changing customer demands. Yet higher sensitivity to the threat often makes these firms tense up in the face of adversity and forget what made them successful in the first place. Many or all of the above problems then surface, setting off a self-reinforcing decline cycle.

A surprising and challenging conclusion of the study just mentioned is that, in comparisons between growing, stable, and declining organizations, problems more typically associated with decline were also present in stable organizations. In fact, no difference in the degree of internal divisiveness was found between stable and declining organizations. Only growing organizations were spared the difficulty of dealing with increasing centralization, conflict, turnover, and resistance to change, a lack of long-term planning, decreasing innovation, and loss of morale.

A recent study of corporate renewal strategies in the steel service industry done for the Steel Service Center Institute (MacMillan, Low, and Starr, 1988) discovered that the pattern of poor performance and increased internal divisiveness was broken only by firms deciding to aggressively pursue a new strategy. In this study, firms that pursued a specialization or diversification strategy did best at overcoming the liability of age. Specialization paid off both in higher returns on assets and in higher growth than comparable firms. And diversification resulted in comparatively higher growth.

The challenge confronting entrepreneurial and closely held companies at the crossroads is this: grow, or face the debilitating problems of decline. While survivability depends to some extent on stability and caution (for example, being alert to high inventory levels), growth is worth seeking for survival's sake too.

We value business growth because it is the source of new jobs, increased wealth, individual development, and—in family firms—family cohesion and health. Sound growth is also the best source of improvement in the survival capacity of a business. But not all growth does this. Examples of growth in the "fast lane" abound in Silicon Valley. Osborne Computer, for example, grew until it died at age five. Osborne was financially and organizationally overextended.

Growth seems to be one of those paradoxical qualities that are best in process, not as an end in themselves. Like love, wealth, and happiness, growth often vanishes when sought directly and feverishly. With both eyes on growth, management has no vision for objectives that are important to survival and growth: quality of product, customer satisfaction, competitiveness, profitability— qualities that may have propelled the entrepreneurial or family business's growth in the first place. So as we consider stimulating business growth in the pages ahead, it is important to envision growth not as a goal in itself, and not as a prerequisite to bigness, but as the best source of energy for business, family, and individual survival, fun, and development.

There are, of course, business owners who want to remain in business and have it provide a good life-style but who are not interested in the problems inherent in growth. They can probably succeed in their efforts only if their expectations span a single generation. Beyond the average twenty-five- or thirty-year product cycle that parallels a generation of management, survival depends on revitalization and growth.

Stages in a Business's Life

Entrepreneurial organizations have a dismal record of preserving the spirit that started them and nurtured them through maturity. This is partially a result of predictable challenges faced by businesses as they age. But while taxes are a certainty, death is not a preordained feature of organizations. Regeneration is very much within the realm of what is humanly possible in businesses. The

Marriott Corporation, Mars, Inc., S. C. Johnson and Son, and others discussed throughout this book provide dramatic evidence of this capability.

And yet the business failure statistics tell us that for every one of these success stories, there are three businesses that failed to survive beyond the first generation (Danco, 1975). What went wrong? Were there any warning signs? Could anything have been done differently to reverse the decline? Research into the history of organizations has identified a somewhat predictable pattern of stages in a business's life (Hershon, 1975; Adizes, 1979; Mintzberg and Waters, 1982). Organizations move from their creation or birth into a period of accelerated growth, which then yields to business rationalization and maturity. At this latter stage, the propensity toward a no-growth and decline stage becomes quite powerful. But stimulated by a new vision (see Figure 1), often articulated by a new generation of managers or owners, the business can be regenerated and management can chart a new path toward a new stage of growth and development.

During the creation/birth stage of a business, innovation, experimentation, risk taking, and passion are almost assured as the entrepreneur, single-handedly or with one or two associates, lines up money from banks, relatives, friends, and/or venture capitalists. The entrepreneur may also play a part in developing the product, manufacturing it for less, customizing it, marketing it in a new and unusual way, or all of the above. At this stage, the goal of short-term survival is paramount in the founder-entrepreneur's mind. Growth seems far in the future. And then suddenly the founder discovers that growth is the very next stage and that the need for it arrived with yesterday's air-express letter: "GM's Buick-Oldsmobile-Canada Division hereby authorizes the purchase of *50,000 quick-connects. . . .*"

As the business accelerates into growth, founders and entrepreneurs face strategic issues about the quality of this development. Is the business growing in knowledge, sophistication, and the quality of the products it makes, markets, or distributes, or is it growing only in volume and size? Is volume growth of quick-connects what the founder wanted to do with his or her life? And because the founder can no longer do it all, who should now lead

Figure 1. Vision—The Catalyst of Smart Growth.

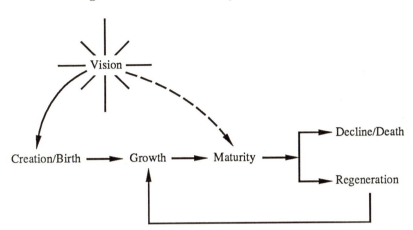

the manufacturing function? Who will stay on top of the finances? These developmental needs of the business trigger internal competition among employees and among family members and raise the specter of nepotism, favoritism, and inequity. By the time the business accelerates along its growth curve, the next generation is often in college or waiting in the wings. This already complex stage is then further complicated by intergenerational family dynamics, sibling rivalries, the reluctance of heirs, and issues of equity between working and passive owners.

Maturity, the next stage, is sometimes wise but decidedly not easy. Under the veneer of wealth, plenty, and "having arrived" (so prevalent in this stage) lies the greatest risk of unperceived and protracted decline and death. At this stage, the business has become a much more complex set of "entitled" constituencies: the banks that have financed the growth, investors, community groups, city government, family members, nonfamily employees. And all these constituencies want different things from the business: timely debt repayment, capital appreciation, contributions, taxes, dividends, and good salaries and career opportunities. These demands all cost the business money and time, and promoting renewed growth also demands plenty of both. What is often left out of consideration by these multiple constituencies is the clear vision that existed when the business was young. The difficulty of successfully meeting the multiple demands of maturity, in the absence of a vision of the future, typically sets the stage for decline.

For some founders and entrepreneurs, the maturity stage is the culmination of a productive single-generation venture: they have no future plans for the business. Most, however, look across the crossroads at the dangers of the decline stage and wonder whether their goal of a healthy family business was only a dream. Of those, some realize that they must sponsor the legacy across generations through a nonfamily, but nevertheless vital, business entity.

But if the business and the family remain reasonably healthy, the business's needs for additional capital for revitalization may be met by refinancing the business. The sale or closure of parts of the company can help, as can the recruitment of professional nonfamily managers to help the family turn the business around. Once decline sets in, however, options disappear and owners are often permitted only the outright sale of the business or its assets, piece by piece.

Early Warning Signs of Decline

By the time that the sales volume slumps and profitability is suffering, decline may be well entrenched. Fortunately, other available information can alert management before too much damage is done to the survival capability of the firm. Here are ten early warning signs:

Sales growth has slowed down. Bottom lines are a lagging indicator of organizational effectiveness. By the time a company shows a deficit, the resulting sense of urgency is probably too little too late. However slight a sales growth slowdown may look at the time, it often means competition and should be heeded as a warning. Young, small competitors have a habit of growing fast.

Looking at dollars rather than units or unit growth is a dangerous business. (The reverse, of course, is also true.)

Profit margins are falling. Management can so narrowly focus its attention on unit growth numbers that it deemphasizes profit margins (the opposite mistake to ignoring sales growth slow-

specific manner. [The president] would advise him of the financial reports he intended to present to the board and the treasurer would bend his figures to suit the [president's] figures" (p. 71).

The board of directors is engaged in face-saving and rubber-stamping behavior. The Curtis-Bok family, controlling owners of Curtis Publishing and the *Saturday Evening Post,* played an absentee-owner role on their board. Both family members and their appointed outsiders (nonfamily and nonmanagement members of the board) were uninformed about and inactive in the business and its performance. They effectively rubber-stamped top-management decisions. Although misinformation from management may have contributed to the board's doing nothing, in the final analysis it was the passive role of the directors that allowed early warning signs and declining performance to occur without confrontation. The firm's problems remained unaddressed.

Worse yet, as problems were identified and acted on by new presidents with fresh perspectives, board support for these initiatives wavered. Because committed support could open board members to accusations of earlier inaction, they engaged in further face-saving behavior.

The recommendations of study teams, task forces, and consultants are being ignored. A lack of honesty about the problems and facts confronting the corporation makes the achievement of improvements impossible. Frequently, the problems being faced by a business are widely known or suspected by a significant number of its employees. Thus opening the lines of communication laterally and vertically is essential to honestly facing the problems in a company. Task forces and study teams are an excellent idea, but implementation of their recommendations is essential. Toyota in Japan continues to receive approximately one million improvement suggestions each year from its employees—not because it has quality circles but because it implements 94 percent of those recommendations.

Employee surveys, study teams, outside consultants, operation auditors, and responsible internal trouble-shooters all offer the possibility of discovering what is really going on in a declining business. If the resulting breaches of the trapped-management system are not acted on immediately, the bureaucracy will protect

enters the picture and influences what is happening in the business and, of course, in the family. In entrepreneurial businesses where the family is not involved, this influence may be delayed until the next generation of management has "earned its stripes" and become a contender for top-management jobs.

In family businesses, the next generation often enters the business at age twenty-four or twenty-five (after an MBA or maybe a couple of years working outside the family business). By the time they are thirty-two or thirty-three, the business's growth has often slowed down. The founder has also slowed down, but the next generation is raring to go. How the founder and the next generation resolve the conflicts brought on by being so out of phase with each other will largely determine whether the business declines a little or a lot, or is regenerated successfully. The context for this generational crisis is provided by technology, the economy, and market waves that present new risks (which the founder perceives) and new opportunities (which the next generation perceives).

Internal to the firm are the differences in age and maturity, experience in business, and critical formative frameworks (for example, the Depression versus the Vietnam War, a modest versus well-off upbringing, and so on) between the generations. These differences are then magnified in family-owned businesses by relationships between subsets of two or three family members who cluster like constellations. This differentiation is, in the long term, quite supportive of the development of healthy individuals but makes the task of managing the firm that much more complex during the next generation's thirties. These are the "talking-back and speaking-up" years. Differences such as these make father, mother, daughter, and son perceive situations very differently, and all concerned experience a lot of conflict. Exacerbating the conflict is the young people's perception that the difference in power between the generations is significant. Even families with good conflict-resolution skills experience difficulties at this stage.

Summary

The biggest risk to a business at the decline-or-regenerate crossroads is that it will sink into decline, mired in inaction.

2

Alternatives to Business Decline: Four Choices

At the crossroads, choose growth. That is the storyline behind this book. But what does that entail? Choosing growth starts with calling for a vision. It then requires an honest assessment of the present conditions of the family business in light of the desired future contained in that vision. Choosing growth further requires that the goals of the business and the family be matched and the results of this match be fused into a coherent strategy for the business. It then requires managing the regeneration state by creating structures and methods that align the organization to the new strategy, and putting in place managerial practices that promote continued entrepreneurial activity across generations. This is the roadmap for this book, as can be seen in Figure 2.

Arriving at a collective decision about the future of the family business—a strategic consensus—is a significant challenge. Although in the early years the entrepreneur often made decisions and acted single-handedly, more people are now involved. The CEO's leadership is still key in making a better choice at the crossroads. But in order to lead well, CEOs have to translate their intuition into words and communicate it to others. They must also listen to and be influenced by what others think.

Figure 2. At the Crossroads: Choosing Growth.

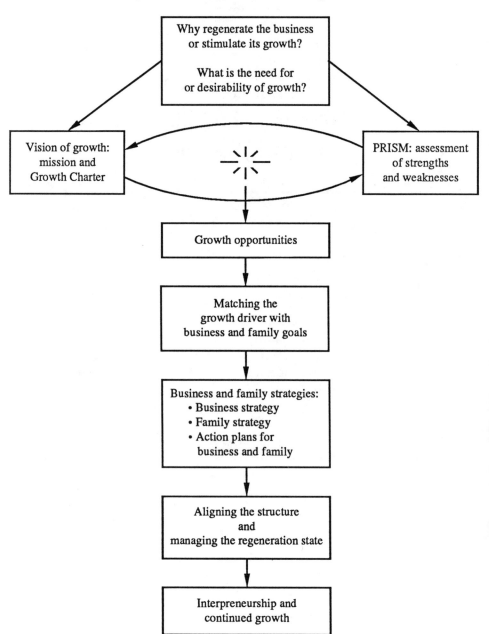

Well-founded commitment to growth is based on a good answer to the question, Why regenerate the business or stimulate its growth? Before prematurely choosing growth, it is appropriate to review other alternatives to decline available at the crossroads. As was stated in the previous chapter, the basic choices are to sell, maintain, or grow the family business. Deciding which one is appropriate for the CEO, the business, and the family will depend on a variety of factors.

Deciding to Sell the Family Business

If decline has set in, a decision to sell before the equity or net worth of the business is destroyed may be quite appropriate. While it is always easier to recognize the attractiveness of this choice in hindsight, the answer to several questions should help evaluate it in the present. Would it be much easier for outsiders to turn the company around? Is the current CEO or the next generation willing to take on one of the hardest tasks in business management—that is, to reverse the decline of a business from within? Does leadership have the ability to do that? Is the next generation of management or family reluctant? Can the family estate benefit from some diversification? Discussing these questions with others generally proves valuable. One person's assessment will almost certainly be affected by blind spots; we all have them.

The further the business has gone into decline, the higher the discount from fair market value it is likely to command on the sale. Businesses for sale are most often valued as going concerns, not as a collection of hard assets. After all, you are not selling the business to the IRS. Selling before earnings, projected earnings, and net worth have gone into decline is smart. (Consultation with business brokers, trade associations, and certified professionals is highly recommended for those considering selling. Business valuation is a very complex and constantly changing subject and not the subject of this book.)

It may also be appropriate to sell a business if competition is intensifying and the will or the ability to fight it out is waning. As the Japanese, intent on capturing foreign markets, have been willing to shrink profit margins on products exported to the United

20

States, many
In other fir
manufactu
lack the
when lar
product v
and thin
           If
valuatic
When
busine
indus
inves
neur
dive
of t
coi
wl
b
g
(

the family with the ability to diversify the estate. Sonesta, for example, trades publicly but is controlled by the Sonnabend family. A diversified estate is particularly important if ownership is becoming more dispersed but the operating company itself is not diversified. Why? Because the differing needs of a growing list of owners may tear away at the fabric of the firm.

In the last several years, many entrepreneurs have taken their companies public in order to raise money to implement changes in production, sales, distribution, or customer service—this with the expectation of becoming more competitive and thereby achieving faster growth. They have essentially decided to take the business out of the family and make it a single-generation affair. Fast-growth companies in industries requiring significant amounts of capital for growth—computer software, for example—have done this successfully. (Going public as a means of raising capital is discussed in considerable detail in Resource A at the end of the book.)

If selling equity to the public is being seriously considered, it is worth keeping in mind that a gradual progression from going public to complete liquidation of the privately held equity is a frequent pattern. Entrepreneurs in search of capital for growth sometimes decide to go public but retain control. That decision often leads, years later, to selling the family business outright—the culmination of a series of decisions called for by the new circumstances. Pressure from analysts or shareholders for short-term results, the public exposure of any mistakes, and the often increased value of the equity after a period of equity-financed growth may drive these decisions.

Several introspective questions may be appropriate in order to determine whether going public is appropriate for a given family business or whether it will inexorably lead to exiting the business, which may not be the most attractive choice.

1. Is the CEO interested in keeping the operating business in the family? Is anybody in the next generation of the family interested in and capable of running the business?
2. Is the CEO the kind of person who, having taken the firm public, could resist the pressures for short-term results and the fluctuation in the price of shares?

3. Is the CEO the kind of person who is willing and able to ignore Wall Street's demand for constant increases in sales and earnings in pursuit of longer-term objectives for the company?
4. Does the CEO function well under the spotlight of analysts and the media? What will the CEO do when mistakes no longer remain private?
5. What is the vision for the future of the CEO? Of the family? Of key top management?
6. What are the prospects for the industry as a whole?
7. Is the CEO still deriving personal satisfaction from the management and ownership of the business?
8. Are all the family assets tied up in the business?

The following is a very partial list of drawbacks to going public: the possibility of a hostile takeover, the potential loss of the entrepreneurial edge (which was maintained by a shoestring operation) when all the equity capital rolls in, the need for consensus among a larger number of constituencies (shareholders, bankers, managers, analysts, family members), and extensive reporting requirements to the SEC and others in government. So while the prospect of going public and retaining control may feel like having the best of both worlds, it may in reality complicate the business and set it on the path to liquidation.

Those considering going public should also keep in mind future career prospects for family members under the new ownership structure. If anybody in the family plans to stay involved in the business beyond the sale of the stock, that decision should influence who the buyer is.

Deciding to Maintain the Business

It is not easy for businesses that are in a maintenance mode— what is also called a holding strategy—to escape the risks of a self-reinforcing decline cycle. Unless the maintenance period is the pause between growth spurts that promotes healthy consolidation, or competition within the industry is benign, to grow or to perish seems to be the choice. This certainly appears to have been Donald Burr's attitude regarding People Express's growth. The irony in that case—in hindsight, of course—is that critics now argue that Burr pushed growth so relentlessly that the absence of maintenance periods doomed the airline. The absence of transitions and time to build systems and practices that would support the next growth spurt overextended the airline's financial and human resources (Hackman, 1986). While Donald Burr did not get excited about the maintenance mode, the organization *needed* some maintenance time for its own survival.

There is also some evidence (Harrigan, 1985) that businesses that are smart enough to choose a small, focused market niche and fortunate enough not to have that niche disturbed by competition or market and technical forces survive across the generations without stimulating growth. Even if leather industrial belting, for example, becomes largely extinct with the advent of metal conveyor systems, there will always be a need for a few specialized applications of leather belting. And after most suppliers of leather belting close their doors in anger at the advent of metal conveyor lines, one or two leather belting makers will have the market all to themselves. Near-monopolies are wonderful news for profit margins and the bottom line. Certainly maintenance, especially during the many years when consolidation in the industry is occurring, is not easy or profitable. But some businesses, especially family businesses, have made it work for them.

J. E. Rhoads and Sons, Inc., is a Pennsylvania tannery that makes leather belting for use in machinery and conveyor belts. Th business was started in 1702 and is still owned and operated by th same family. In 1985 it had annual sales of about $5 million. Th decision to maintain the business was based on the followi continued family interest in working the business (although in mid 1970s a lapse occurred when none of the three members o next generation had yet joined the firm; a daughter has jo since), clarity by the Rhoads family about the firm's market satisfaction with this niche and its lack of growth, and family that consider the business more a means to the end of public and family well-being than an end in itself. According to members, the company was never especially interested in cation or expansion, an attitude they attribute to the Quaker religion.

carried on for a long period of time—say, over three years—maintenance tends to give rise to many of the same problems inherent in decline: lowered employee morale, resistance to change, divisiveness, and customer dissatisfaction with the cost-reduction efforts inherent in the maintenance decision.

Deciding to Grow

Maturity is the trickiest of business stages. Beneath the veneer of wealth, success, power, and plenty lies the risk of hidden and protracted decline and death. The business's set of "entitled" constituencies—the banks that have financed the growth, investors, community groups that have learned to depend on the business's largesse, city government, family members, and nonfamily employees and their families—all want different things from the business. These cost money, leadership attention, and time. And promoting regeneration and growth also demands plenty of each. The difficulty in successfully meeting this complex constellation of demands creates an emotionally charged and resource-constrained context for CEOs, who have to deal with successors, relatives, and employees as well as reconcile the work's demands and rewards with the goals they have for the rest of their own lives. Is this the reward founders and second-generation CEOs get for having worked so hard, for having built a thriving business? It is hard to disagree with some founders' sense that there is no fairness in this world, that nobody out there is listening, and that nobody out there cares.

Handling all of these conflicts is not management's only task, however. The CEO must also remain vigilant to signs of decline. How many of the early warning signs are present in the business? Slowdown of combined unit sales and revenue growth? Eroding profit margins? Widespread fudging of the numbers and a diet of only good news? Face-saving or rubber-stamping behavior by the board of directors, "kitchen cabinet," or circle of friends and advisers? An overemphasis on bureaucratic procedures and routines and an increasing number of employees in staff jobs? Lack of vision and focus?

The large and proud Curtis-Bok family-owned publisher ceased to exist about twenty-five years after unsuccessfully resolving a crisis at the crossroads. But the Curtis-Bok family enterprise need not have died. It is in the best interest of visionary entrepreneurs, committed founders, next-generation CEOs of family-controlled businesses, family members, employees, owners/stockholders, communities, and the U.S. economy as a whole that businesses live across generations. When they fail to do so, the waste of human energy and financial capital is irrational, immoral, and unacceptable.

Let us now turn to two examples of companies that survived—and thrived—as they grew across generations. Theirs are success stories of smart growth.

A good example of the benefits of regeneration in a family business is M. Jacobs and Sons, a bottle manufacturer and distributor in Detroit that has been revitalized by every single generation. Its founder built a business around recycling used glass bottles in the late 1800s, at a time when bottles were handblown and expensive. The second generation started entering the business in 1915, and by the early 1920s the growing firm distributed to the largest beverage manufacturers and bottlers in the United States.

When the third generation of entrepreneurs took over the business, they decided to add plastic bottles to their distribution capability, as plastic bottles were rapidly gaining favor with bottlers. One generation later, even this venture had become old hat and profit margin–shy. So in the early 1980s, the fourth generation decided to go directly to retail customers with new plastic bottles. The new division formed to support the pursuit of this vision today sells plant-misters to K-Marts, nurseries, and drugstore chains nationwide (Posner, 1985).

A supermarket chain in the Northeast, now a second-generation family business, appears headed for similar growth across generations. The third generation is creating new but related businesses that may have a regenerative impact on the parent company. The two third-generation brothers have started related businesses in which their family-derived knowledge of the market and of the internal operations of the food retailing business gives them an edge.

The elder brother founded a specialty food retailer that emphasizes service to busy executives and professionals in several major metropolitan areas. The stores are being franchised na-

for the company. They restructured the organization to support greater customer orientation in the stores and made changes in their sibling behavior to increase the effectiveness of their shift toward greater customer orientation at headquarters.

The need for these changes was far from obvious to the brothers; they were too close to the problem to see it. But the eldest, the current president, was not getting what he wanted from the organization in either advertising copy or product availability in the stores, areas of responsibility headed by the two younger siblings. The president called in a consultant to conduct an organizational review of the operation.

After much discussion and a significant amount of shuttle diplomacy between brothers by the consultant, a consensus emerged about the need to change the organizational structure and the roles and responsibilities of the brothers. These changes, it was hoped, would result in corresponding changes in sibling behaviors that were causing frustration and disharmony in the family and in the business.

Midwest Electronics developed a new mission statement that focused the business on value-added customer service, following a strategic redirection called for by a recent customer study. Midwest Electronics also regionalized the retail operations, thereby reducing a layer of headquarters retail staff and changing the role of the store manager (who was previously almost drowned in paperwork) to emphasize sales and customer-service activities. Finally, they gave overall responsibility for retail stores to the very able and motivated youngest brother. He had previously been second-guessing every decision made by the nonfamily retail operations manager.

In their changes of strategy, organization, and family behavior, the brothers have purposefully taken steps to bring about changes in both the family and the firm that support growth and interpreneurship.

Strategic Exploration. Through strategic exploration, a business can focus on its mission, examine its strengths and weaknesses relative to the competition, and map its future accordingly. Such management initiatives concerning strategy are often led by a successor to the founder-entrepreneur, acting as strategy czar. Strategic analysis and planning naturally tap the future orientation of the next generation and may increase the entrepreneurial propensity of the founder. However, even an entrepreneurial and intuitive founder may have difficulties supporting or participating in strategic planning if this process is forced upon him by an aggressive, forward-looking second generation. It is important for the second generation to be sensitive to the needs of the founder at this late stage of his life (Lansberg, 1988). Framing the interpreneurial effort as a natural progression that builds on the founder's legacy and acknowledges the contribution that the founder has made may ease the transition to the next phase of growth.

Organizational Change and Development. Changes in strategy are often accompanied by changes in structure, and vice versa. The objective in changing the structure in growth-seeking businesses is to provide enough autonomy to the various product, business, technological, or geographical units to allow them to operate with plenty of exposure to the competitive environment. The intent is to have new ventures operate as if in a free-market environment. Some of these innovative organizational approaches also help institutionalize the process of growth.

In family-owned businesses, other possible objectives of structural reorganization include the fostering of managerial skills in successors and the reduction of conflicts between potential successors (often siblings) or between founder and successor. The firm is split into separate functional areas, divisions, or geographical regions, each headed by different family (and perhaps some nonfamily) managers.

But there is more to organization than structure. Some firms create new communication and coordination mechanisms, such as quarterly business review meetings for the family. Other businesses emphasize management development of owners and other organizational members. A family business may also negotiate role changes that allow greater differentiation of roles within the business and the family. (Differentiation between such roles is essential.)

Other organizational development approaches used to promote continued growth include steering committees, asset boards, an outside board of directors, in-house management education of

Table 2. Financial Restructuring Options, Cont'd.

Financial Restructuring Technique	*What It Is*
Employee stock ownership plan (ESOP)	An IRS-qualified stock bonus or stock purchase plan designed to encourage employers to give or sell stock to their employees through a trust, in exchange for tax advantages in the treatment of capital gains and the costs of borrowing to finance the transaction. ESOPs can thus help ensure that the business is carried on by people committed to its survival and prosperity.

even more frequently, lack of consensus about how to get there, often subjects the business to prolonged periods of paralysis, during which no interpreneurial activity is possible.

Family culture may also decree the extent of differentiation among family members: between parents and offspring, and among the siblings themselves. For example, a son or daughter may have a difficult struggle establishing his or her own leadership style and worldview while working under the shadow of a parent who is also a boss. To the extent that principles of equality overshadow each individual's unique abilities and strengths, individuation and role differentiation among siblings may be difficult to achieve. These obstacles, in turn, often blunt the interpreneurial potential of next-generation family members, because they interfere with the individual's ability to harness his or her energy and creativity. Thus changing the family system is often a prerequisite to interpreneuring and continued growth.

Summary

Decline is the choice by default. There are much better alternatives at the crossroads of a business's life. Selling the business, going public, employing a maintenance/holding strategy to build a foundation for the next growth leg, and growth are all better choices.

Why sell the business?

- Because it is easier for "outsiders" to turn a declining business around
- Because the family estate could benefit from diversification and liquidity
- Because competition is intensifying and the will or ability to fight it out is waning
- Because new technology may be changing the rules of the game or making the firm's offerings obsolete or too costly
- Because a large firm with "marketing muscle" may have decided to get into the same line of business
- Because money transfers more easily to the next generation than the will and ability to continue the business

Preparation for the sale is essential. It is wise to consult trade associations and business valuation experts. Preparing a portfolio on the business, much as a business broker would do if retained to sell the business, is useful. Leveraged buy-outs and employee stock ownership plans are currently popular approaches to selling the family business.

Why go public?

- Because it provides additional capital for growth
- Because it helps diversify the family estate
- Because selling some of the equity can provide funds for growth, diversification, or liquidity, while allowing continued control of the corporation

But can the CEO resist the pressures for short-term results and the impact these expectations have on fluctuations in the price of the stock? Does the family want to keep the business in the family? What is the vision for the future?

Drawbacks to going public include the following: the possibility of a hostile takeover, potential loss of the entrepreneurial edge because of the sudden large influx of equity capital at the time of the sale of equity, and extensive reporting requirements.

Why maintain the business?

the family business commitment plan, which can help replace lack of information (and resulting overcautiousness) with a reawakened commitment by the owning family to revitalizing the business.

Chapter Six elaborates on the crafting of business strategy as the single most important contributor to managing the growth effort. Business strategy that is responsive to the cumulative wisdom of the current generation, the dreams of the next, a thorough competitive analysis, and an appraisal of overall economic, political, and social conditions is good strategy.

In Chapter Seven I examine the necessity for aligning the structure of the organization with the chosen strategy. Businesses need vision, but they also need to be able to pursue this vision without undue hardship. I discuss restructuring through widespread use of teams, changing traditional family patterns that are no longer helpful, and creating new capital structures, new compensation systems, and active review boards.

3

The Process of Smart Growth and How to Stimulate It

In this age of business breakthroughs and company transformations, it is often difficult to remember this fact: growth is always taking place in healthy individuals and healthy organizations. Sure, the growth process ebbs and flows, spurts and sputters, sprints and pauses; but it is always there, in some part of the business, from birth to death.

The dynamic process of growth is different at different stages of the business's life. Business growth researchers (Cohn and Lindberg, 1974; Adizes, 1979) suggest that during the firm's first stage—birth and short-term survival—growth is focused on customers and markets. Later in the cycle, such internal considerations as morale and human resource development take prominence in the growth agenda. Management may turn next to internal planning and control and the development of goal setting and management information systems. Eventually, the focus is on the acquisition of greater resources for further growth, which may trigger a beginning of this cycle all over again.

Each of the significant movements in the ongoing process of growth is experienced as a major and often traumatic transition for the business and the people managing it. The early stages of rebirth, for instance, are often perceived not as growth-filled but as lacking growth. Growth feels awkward, and in the beginning and middle of

could commit immediately. It did. The second statement was made by Sam Steinberg, chairman of Steinberg Inc., a diversified supermarket chain headquartered in Montreal.

The two orientations are obviously quite different. Donald Burr is hooked on growth—any growth—and appears to have little appreciation for the need for pauses and transitions in the process of growing. Sam Steinberg, on the other hand, believes in sending probes into the future through a growth spurt and then taking time to catch a breath before growing some more. This is, in fact, the pattern of growth exhibited by Steinberg, Inc., throughout its seventy-year history. M. Jacobs and Sons, the family-owned Detroit bottle manufacturer mentioned in Chapter Two, has experienced similar cycles; in their case, these have been aligned with the rise of a new generation of family business owners.

These cycles, in the aggregate, used to take approximately forty years, but they appear to be shortening. Cycles of about twenty years seem to be predominating now in the oscillation between development and the exploitation of development represented by the move from birth (startup) to maturity to early decline (Ward, 1987). For a particular company, the cycle may of course be shorter or longer, depending on its industry's maturity and competitive dynamics. Because the average tenure of one generation is twenty-four years, this may ultimately mean that rebirths will have to be promoted more than once during a generation's tenure in the business. It may also imply that smaller growth successes have to be planned and implemented more frequently within the major twenty- or twenty-five-year cycle if the business is going to remain healthy.

Assessing Energy for Growth

Borrowing from David Gleicher's change formula (Beckhard and Harris, 1987), we can look at *energy for growth* (EG) as being the result of (1) *dissatisfaction* with the status quo (D), often a holding or maintaining strategy; (2) the *vision* (V) of growth, including concrete accomplishments within targeted timeframes; and (3) specific steps to *get started* (GS) on the road to growth. In order for the growing process to begin, enough of each of these components needs to be present, and their combined force needs to be greater than the intensity of the natural *forces of decline* (FD) discussed in Chapter Two. In other words,

$$EG = D \times V \times GS \gg FD$$

If any one of the three energy-producing components is not present in sufficient quantities, growth will languish no matter how much of each of the other components in the formula is present. In other words, because it is a multiplicative function, if any of the factors approaches zero, energy for growth will be reduced to zero.

The implications of this formula for CEOs interested in stimulating growth and for practitioners committed to helping family businesses grow are the following:

1. Diagnose the business and family situation to discover the strength of each of these components and therefore the available energy for growth.
2. Work on increasing the factor that is least present in the current situation, because it offers the highest payback.
3. Reduce or eliminate the forces of decline. These often reflect well-established patterns, and their elimination represents a personal cost to individual family members, the CEO who is "holding on," the siblings who find it impossible to agree, and others. If this is not done, however, the situation may become further polarized and "stressed," with growth and decline forces both gathering intensity.

Dissatisfaction with the status quo (D), the first factor in our energy-for-growth formula, is an important source of energy for growth. Most companies seem to allow this dissatisfaction to be felt only after it reaches crisis proportions—for example, when competitors begin winning over preferred customers, or after sales have declined sharply and profits have taken a nosedive.

The secret of high-performing companies is their ability to confront potential difficulties *before* the marketplace, with its long time-lag, has finally done so. Focusing the organization on an honest assessment of where it stands stimulates creative tension between where the firm is and where it wants to be. Knowing this, dedicated people can begin to engage in the collective process of narrowing the gap by reshaping the present in the image of the vision.

Activities that help create this sense of urgency, so naturally prevalent in young entrepreneurial companies, are plentiful:

- The implementation of new information systems that openly communicate, throughout the organization, labor costs, scrap and waste costs, inventory costs, quality indices, and information on competitors and their performance
- The use of consultants, with their more objective external perspective
- Visits to high-performing entrepreneurial companies in similar industries
- Changes in compensation and reward systems

A vision of growth (V) that is rich in detail and represents what is truly wanted by the CEO and the owning family is the second important component of our formula. An attractive vision of the future creates a pull toward a more desirable future and heightens the healthy dissatisfaction with the status quo (D).

Even with plenty of healthy dissatisfaction with the status quo (D) and a compelling vision (V) of a desired future, energy for growth (EG) will not exceed the natural forces of decline (FD) without practical steps that get the firm started on the road to realizing its vision. The management-of-change literature notes that these steps need to be taken before "refreezing takes place" (Lewin, 1943; Kurt Lewin's model of change stipulates that there is an unfreezing, a changing, and a refreezing stage to every change). Many cases of failed management of change reflect a missed opportunity to get started (GS) at internal organizational change to cope with external change. It is not long after such a missed opportunity that the bureaucratic forces that promote a steady state again get the upper hand and inappropriately stabilize the organization as if nothing requiring change had happened. Practical first steps are needed before the sense of urgency dissipates and the energy for growth fades.

Here is an example of a crossroads company in which the energy-for-growth formula provided the consultant to the family business with insights into appropriate interventions and into appropriate behaviors by the company's CEO.

The unexpected death of this southwestern company's founder shook the family to its core. Although estate plans were in order, the emotions unleashed by the founder's heart attack threw everything else into chaos. By the time the consultant was retained a year later, several major decisions had already been made. The youngest member of the second generation, the only one previously employed in the business, emerged as the only one interested in running it. Against the recommendations of all other major shareholders (mother, sister, and brother), the firm's equity was bought by the youngest family member. The purchase was financed jointly by the mother and the only bank they found that agreed to a loan without a personal guarantee.

During the consultant's first visit, several things became clear. First, the successor was running on fear of failure and deep dissatisfaction with the way the business had been managed before. Most of his dissatisfaction was masked, however, because of his own ambivalence at not being appreciative enough of his father, especially now that he was dead. Second, the successor had been in a reactive mode to events in his business and personal life since his father's death. Third, the successor wanted to grow the company, rather than restrain it the way he had seen his father do; he knew that he did not want to do business his father's way.

In other words, D (dissatisfaction with the status quo) was high, but V (vision of desired future) was nonexistent, or at least close to a value of zero in the energy-for-growth formula. In the absence of vision, getting started on the road to growth was a random series of disconnected events.

As a result of this diagnosis, the consultant took it on himself to initiate discussions with the successor and his wife. These eventually helped develop a vision that was exclusively the province of this second-generation family. In the process, the consultant talked often with each of the two family members, separately and together; recorded these conversations on paper and on flip charts; periodically drafted, and then finalized, a six-page mission-and-vision document for the firm and the family.

The CEO and the consultant also planned actions that would communicate to everyone in the organization the commitment to the new vision. In carefully orchestrated ways, the CEO selected a few powerfully symbolic new behaviors—behaviors that he believed in and that he also believed would communicate at least part of his new vision more loudly than words. The new CEO began parking his car in the employee lot, on a first-come, closest to the building basis (message: "We are in this together"); he sold a massive old piece of equipment that had been idle and used the proceeds to buy a smaller but very efficient injection molding machine (message: "Machine utilization is important; we will reinvest in the business to improve"); and he instituted quarterly state-of-the-company meetings with employees (message: "Communication is important"). And not forgetting the power of words as well as actions, the CEO also began calling all employees associates. The CEO/consultant team had successfully homed in on that firm's two lowest contributors to energy for growth in the business: vision, and steps for getting started on the road to growth.

Each of the first three factors, if present in a large enough quantity, has the capability of aligning people and their energies toward the pursuit of growth. The forces of decline, on the other hand, have the ability to break up and deflect energies, thereby creating conflict and raising the ante in the decision to grow. Decline forces were at a minimum in this case, because of the crisis that had precipitated the succession and the mother's and siblings' decision to sell their shares to the new CEO. Other circumstances could call for more activity aimed at reducing these forces.

Increasing Energy for Growth

Management can foster energy for growth through certain activities.

Symbolic Behavior by the CEO. Both the family and the business need to adopt behaviors that signal a change. Some leaders accomplish this through the change of simple but highly visible routines, as the CEO did with his parking in the case just described. Others signal change by pulling together information on the situation that concerns them, focusing people's attention on it, and thereby orchestrating "crisis conditions" and fostering dissatisfaction with the status quo. Leaders can also be powerful role models of growth by realigning their own work-focus. For instance, CEOs might spend more of their time on the firm's engineering and product development activity if growth through technology is desired.

Problem-Solving Meetings. Involving employees in problem solving is a powerful intervention for new leadership, a unique opportunity to open up channels of communication and create a sense of urgency. The new owners of a midwestern manufacturing firm started their second year of ownership by hosting an "open-ear" problem-finding meeting for all employees. They also sponsored the formation of problem-solving teams throughout the company. Some of these teams addressed customer complaints; others, manufacturing problems; still others, human resource issues. Problem identification and problem solving became part of everyone's job.

Education. Education in problem-solving skills, statistical process control (SPC), employee involvement concepts, "the big picture" of business, financial management, and change management can foster in managers and owners a greater appreciation for the need to grow and the requirements of growth. While family members active in the business will be exposed to company-offered programs, nonmanaging owners also require plenty of education and communication about the business. Retreats with experts, consultants, and top management are a good way to educate the family.

Hiring of an Organizational Development Consultant. A strategic organization consultant can help translate education and training into the specific developmental challenges of individual managers, the owning family, and the organization. An appreciation for and skill-base in management, systems, and the family (as well as in interpersonal and group processes) are essential in this professional.

Identification of High-Credibility Growth Advocates and the Building of a Critical Mass. The process of growth depends on the support of "early adopters" of the growth agenda. Both in the family and in the business, these early adopters need to be mobilized to start working on key "undecideds," so that a critical mass of growth promoters is formed and the momentum of the growth process is maintained. One way to start mobilizing this critical mass is through open dialogue among family members and business associates on the growth vision for the business.

PRISM: Assessing the Present in Light of the Vision

The CEO needs to focus attention on developing throughout the organization an accurate, honest assessment of the present state of affairs. As has been noted, focusing the organization on an honest assessment of where it stands stimulates creative tension between where the firm is and where it wants to be. The vision of growth stands in stark contrast to present conditions. Seeing this, dedicated people can begin to engage in the collective process of narrowing the gap by building on strengths, shoring up weaknesses, and thus reshaping the present in the image of the vision. CEOs and other senior management have an active role to play in creating the kind of "crisis environment" that leads to this unsettling reappraisal.

One technique that has proven helpful in honestly assessing the current state of affairs in light of the vision of growth is the PRISM, which breaks a vision's powerful beam of energy into its primary component "colors" of Power, Roles and Responsibilities, Information, Strategy, and Management. (See Figure 3.) While it may seem a little gimmicky, the code word does help people remember the tool and use it in their own regeneration efforts.

Using the analytical tool of the PRISM, an organization can be fine-tuned to pursue its vision. All of the factors in the PRISM framework are linked; therefore, in the present, all are mutually supportive of the current state of affairs. To bring about the change that is required to support a regeneration at the crossroads means

Figure 3. The PRISM Diagnostic.

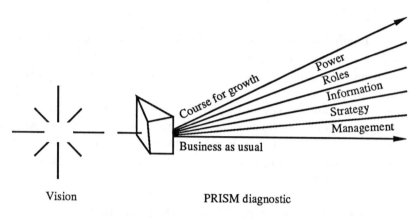

changing one or two of the factors to begin with, and then changing them all in support of the new system, in accordance with the vision.

Assessing an organization's present situation is a complex task. The strength of the PRISM diagnostic lies in its ability to break that task into manageable subtasks. Rather than evaluating the business as a whole, assessors using PRISM diagnose each component separately, asking the following questions as well as others that occur to them.

1. Power
    A. The Company
        • How powerful is the firm relative to its competitors, and where does its competitive advantage lie?
        • Does the company have any "power brands," such as Dixie in paper cups, or Snickers in candy?
        • Is it considered best, or is it top-rated in several of its product categories?
        • Is it the lowest-cost producer, a world-class-quality manufacturer, or the highest in customer service?
    B. Its People
        • How willing is the CEO to share power with the next generation in the interest of a regenerated company?

- How capable are employees of taking action without dozens of approvals to contend with?
- Do employees experience themselves as making a difference, as contributors?

2. Roles and Responsibilities
   - Are owners clear on what their jobs and responsibilities are?
   - Are responsibilities clear for everybody in the company?
   - Does management provide an organizational chart, job descriptions, and/or goals and objectives for individuals and teams?
   - Are responsibilities clear between siblings in the business?
   - Is the business separated by functions or divisions that enable different family members to have their own "turf"?
   - If there are owners who are not active in the business, is their role clear to themselves and others?
   - Is the separation of family and business roles satisfactory to working family members, or do they complain about business issues finding their way to the home and vice versa?

3. Information
   - Do information systems and communication patterns allow people to understand the impact of their decisions? Are they timely?
   - Do these systems help people care about the important details: customer service, quality, costs, competitors' performance?

4. Strategy
   - Is the strategy of the business clear?
   - Is there agreement on it?
   - Is the organization constantly in touch with customers and distributors, and informed of the competition?
   - Are participative management, employee involvement, statistical process control (SPC), or other im-

provement efforts driven by the competitive requirements of the business's strategy?

5. Management
- Is the organizational structure simple, with few layers
  and a lean staff?
- Do task teams, project groups, and business teams
  make the organization feel small and manageable?
- Do all important projects, products, and programs
  have champions?
- Are people respected and treated with integrity?
- Are older, founder-loyal employees willing to work for
  the next generation?
- Are there "atta-boys" and "atta-girls" for jobs well
  done?
- Does pay reward performance, knowledge, and contri-
  butions to productivity, quality, and profitability?
- Are managers really leading people?
- Is senior management helping fuse these five dimen-
  sions of the PRISM into a powerful beam of energy
  aimed at the vision for growth?

Once these and similar questions are answered, the PRISM
will have helped to identify key subsystems that may need changing.
These subsystems are parts of the organization, the family, or the
immediate environment that are affected by or can affect the
changes inherent in the vision. For example, all departmental
managers, the vice-president of marketing, and the compensation
system may be key subsystems affecting movement toward the vision
of growth. Department managers may be key if all personnel
ultimately report to them. The vice-president of marketing may be
important if the vision includes the marketing of a new product line
that he or she is currently negotiating to acquire. And if an
employee survey finds that pay inequities are a major irritant and
are likely to undermine any growth efforts, pay is an important
subsystem.

Arriving at action plans to address the troublesome subsystems appropriately is the challenge of the *regeneration state,* which
will be discussed in Chapter Seven.

Summary

Three areas of activity aimed at stimulating energy for growth and battling the natural forces of decline were highlighted in this chapter: promoting dissatisfaction with the status quo, formulating a vision of growth, and taking steps toward getting started on the road to growth. Companies that have been extremely successful and are still enjoying the image and wealth created ten or twenty years earlier may require that the CEO arrange for a companywide "wake-up call"—and for that matter, a familywide "wake-up call"—before getting started on the road to growth. Energies may need to be mobilized and a sense of urgency forged before any new growth efforts can be launched.

The competitiveness of today's global markets seems to have eliminated most businesses' ability to ignore bad news for any extended period of time. As a result, some previously inner-directed privately held businesses have arranged for adequate exposure to the world outside their community and industry confines through the use of consultants and an active board of directors. Both are extremely helpful in creating or supporting healthy dissatisfaction with the status quo and therefore contribute significantly to energy for growth.

It is worth emphasizing that if healthy dissatisfaction with the status quo is absent in the company and/or the family, this is the place to start. It is very difficult to mobilize the forces of growth for even the most attractive of visions if the present does not leave something to be desired.

While much of this "healthy" dissatisfaction is created by the extremely competitive times we are living in, CEOs can play a part in creating it where it is absent or focusing it where it is dispersed, and acting as a general organizational "depressant." CEOs can then redirect it for positive, growthful activity in the family and the firm.

Steps on the road to growth need to be taken promptly, before the family and business systems renegotiate a new steady state and freeze out any additional growth opportunities.

How can leaders move their organizations forward, keeping eyes and hearts on the vision and their feet firmly planted on the present state of affairs? By actively communicating and revising the vision as others' input is obtained, using the PRISM to assess the present in light of the vision, and beginning to align the organization's priorities with its vision of growth.

"Talking the talk and walking the walk" of the new vision is essential for it to be understood and believed. But commitment to it will generally follow only if the serious exploration of growth opportunities begins. (See Figure 4.) The search for specific growth opportunities that will bring reality to earlier discussions of a growth vision is the subject of the next chapter.

Figure 4. Creating a New Synthesis of Ownership and Management Through Growth.

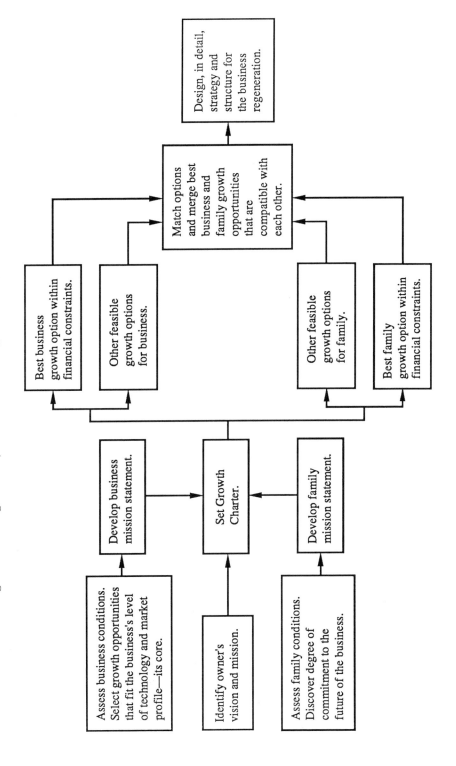

4

Uncovering and Analyzing Growth Opportunities

There are three dominant thrusts available to family businesses planning their growth and regeneration at the crossroads: maintenance, specialization, and diversification.

The first of these, the holding/maintaining thrust, represents little or no growth. Because it can be used to keep decline temporarily at bay, however, it is included as a growth thrust here. Three marginally "growthful" opportunities within the holding/maintaining thrust are cost reduction, pruning/retrenching, and staying put.

The second growth thrust is that of specialization, whether in customers, markets, technologies, or products. Growth opportunities under the specialization thrust include quality or customer-service improvement, new products, increased market share, increased control over the channels of distribution, increased control over suppliers, acquisition of or merger with competitors, and licensing, franchising, and cloning.

A business can diversify—the third and final revitalization thrust—to take advantage of its technical or market expertise, diversify into unrelated business areas, expand geographically, or invest outside the core business.

Only one or two of the growth opportunities summarized above and developed in the rest of the chapter are likely to be appropriate for a particular business. Some will be too expensive.

Others may represent too sharp a departure from what has made the business successful over the years. Still others may require abilities that the owners and employees currently lack or may rely on values that owners cannot support.

The list of opportunities has been organized in keeping with the concept of cautiously moving out from the boundaries of the core business; in other words, earlier ones generally represent a less risky departure than later ones from what has worked in the past. While the first several growth opportunities may not appear as attractive for growth as later ones, growth opportunities have to fit the owners and the company. But before further analyzing the fit, let us explore all the choices. By doing so, we may find that never-before-considered options for growth appear both feasible and attractive. Each of the fifteen options will be submitted to the grueling test in the pages to come. In other words, there will be a chance to "kick the tires."

Holding/Maintaining Thrust

The maintenance thrust places most of its emphasis on improving efficiencies through cost reduction, pruning and re-trenching activity, and staying put. Cost management and necessary maintenance are the focus of managerial activity. The holding/maintaining thrust can be deployed in order to build the manage-rial discipline and conserve the financial resources needed to sponsor future revitalization and growth activity.

Cost Reduction. Reducing costs of manufacture, distribu-tion, or sales opens up a variety of additional opportunities for growth. At the heart of all competitive advantage in the marketplace is the customer's perception of relative value of the product. Perceived value is the difference between the perceived benefits offered by the product or service and its perceived price. I keep using the word *perceived* because, while this perception may very well be based on reality, it may also be a creation of able marketers. The perception of value may be the result of value-added features, lower price, or product differentiation of some sort. A Georgia pencil company, for instance, came back to life after introducing designer colors and patterns to the no-growth business of pencils.

Price reductions, while powerful, are full of risk. They are most perilous when prices are reduced in the marketplace to create a perception of value—but without an immediate reduction in cost. Curtis Publishing reduced prices several times during its almost one hundred-year history. In its later stages of maturity and decline, however, management apparently forgot the direct connection between a pricing tactic and the producer's costs. Margins thus suffered, further undermining the potential for continued growth at Curtis.

Cost reduction, both an art and a science, is not necessarily well understood by owners and managers of firms that have recently emerged from growth and early-maturity periods. On the other hand, many firms in a decline stage have veritable armies of skilled cost-cutters. It may be wise to bring some of these people into the younger firm, but only if there is value or cultural congruency. A cost-cutter whose reputation has been built on people-reduction programs should be avoided if the firm is committed to its employees and their jobs, however. Cost-reduction and margin-improvement opportunities abound in areas less "dangerous" than personnel: inventories, material waste, cash-flow management, and product costing and pricing.

Pruning/Retrenching. In order to take advantage of growth opportunities in one area of the business, it may be necessary for management to prune back parts of the business that have grown beyond their ability to contribute to profitability.

Divesting or selling businesses that no longer produce profits raises cash to finance new growth opportunities elsewhere. Earlier attempts at growth may have failed, and the parts of the business that represent those earlier efforts may need to be eliminated so that one or two healthy product or service lines are not saddled with keeping the losers alive.

In 1979 Rubbermaid, the Ohio manufacturer of plastic products, found itself with only two healthy divisions out of its collection of eight. Realizing that the two divisions could not carry six nonperforming ones, Rubbermaid's new CEO embarked on a retrenchment program that sold off five of its divisions and strengthened one. Between 1979 and 1983, Rubbermaid sold a leading manufacturer of car mats, a diverse industrial products division, and a mobile garbage container division that sold its product to city waste and garbage-handling departments on a bid basis. The cash from these sales was then used to acquire businesses that represented growth opportunities for the two divisions that were already strong. It also permitted the company to explore regional expansion in areas where demographic analysis highlighted potential growth. All acquisitions were congruent with Rubbermaid's established marketing and technical skills. The resulting revitalization of Rubbermaid has been dramatic.

The management of family-owned businesses may also want to take the opportunity to prune back branches of the family that are not supportive of or conducive to the growth of the business. Focusing the business on its core activities after selling, divesting, or eliminating some operations presents opportunities for concentrating ownership on members of the family who are active in the business. The liquidation value of the pruned parts of the business could provide liquidity to owners who are not active in, contributing to, or even interested in the business. Concentrating ownership on those interested in operating the business enhances the chances for survival and growth, as an interesting study of 200 family-owned businesses revealed (Ward, 1987).

Staying Put. There is nothing automatically wrong with staying put to revitalize and grow the business. "Staying put to grow" is not the contradiction it first appears to be. For one thing, a firm's vision of growth may be more qualitative than quantitative; increased numbers and sales growth may not be the ultimate goal. And a foundation for the next growth leg can be built during the pause that a staying-put period affords.

When is staying put appropriate? The market or market niche in which a firm operates may be consolidating; competitors may be closing their doors, reducing the competitive intensity of the industry (and leading to growth and improved margins). In a service or knowledge industry, planned growth may be in reputation, visibility, and influence. Holding the course, not quitting or changing direction, may be the most appropriate operating decision.

The A. J. Canfield Co. of Chicago, which has faced the dilemmas of growth with clarity of purpose, knows the value of staying put. Founded by Arthur Canfield in 1922, the company faced a unique growth opportunity with its new drink, Diet Chocolate Fudge Soda. When sales of this one product skyrocketed in 1985 after a favorable review in a syndicated newspaper column, Art Canfield, his younger brother Alan, and a nonfamily executive vice-president followed the wisdom of their founder and the second-generation owner. They did not immediately seek manufacturing capacity expansion, nor did they consider selling the business or going public while the firm was "hot" in the public's eye. Instead, they decided to decline any new customers. Their reasons? After a couple of months of sixteen-hour workdays and seven-day work-weeks at their plants, employees had started to complain; and customers who had come to depend on Canfield for reliable customer service complained that they were being ignored (Hyatt, 1987).

Their ultimate decision was to sell the drink's concentrate to franchised bottlers so that Canfield could take advantage of the popularity of their Chocolate Fudge without borrowing money to build new plants or going public to finance such expansion. Franchises were not sold, but existing bottlers were approved for bottling the product; the only profit came from sales of the concentrate. Canfield thus decided to stay put as a regional drink manufacturer and bottler. Diet Chocolate Fudge is now available nationally and overseas, but only the syrup is Canfield's except in those areas traditionally served by Canfield: Illinois, Indiana, and Michigan.

Specialization Thrust

The specialization thrust emphasizes the market or technical expertise of the firm and uses that expertise as a unique competitive advantage. Market share in a focused niche is increased through product quality, customer service, new products that exploit the market or technical expertise, and/or the acquisition of competitors or suppliers in the same industry.

Quality or Customer-Service Improvement. Research on strategy and firm performance has highlighted relative quality as a significant contributor to sustainable competitive advantage and profitability. Growth through product quality is a very attractive opportunity for entrepreneurial and family-owned businesses; because their name (and reputation) is on the business, building, and label, they care about quality.

Over the last several years, several family-owned businesses that supply the automotive industry with components and parts have achieved significant growth by working very hard to certify as high-quality preferred suppliers for Ford and GM. A customer-driven search for quality and reliable single-source suppliers has opened significant growth opportunities for many founders and next-generation family-business owners. Intense, caring, and reliable customer service has similarly provided firms that are often local or regional in nature with a growing opportunity.

New Products. Substantial improvement in the performance characteristics of a product or the creation of new products for existing markets (substitution of thermoplastic for glass accessories for microwaves, for instance) presents tremendous opportunities for growth. Creation of new products is a particularly attractive option for established, well-recognized names or brands. Customer loyalty can then be "vested" on its new products.

Raiders and leveraged-buy-out firms often pursue brand-name firms precisely because of their assessment that current management is not aggressively exploiting the competitive strength of the customer loyalty that probably took decades to develop.

Increased Market Share. Through mergers with or acquisitions of competitors, and through pricing, advertising, and merchandising or product development that creates product differentiation, a business can increase its share of a particular market niche. If pricing is considered a key competitive lever, cost-reduction efforts should accompany—or better yet, precede—price reductions.

Significant market shares (38 percent plus) have been shown to be positively correlated with firm profitability (Shoeffler, Buzzell, and Heany, 1974). This research on market shares and profitability is often misunderstood, however. It should not encourage entrepreneurial and family-owned businesses to compete head to head with General Electric across a broad-spectrum market segment. On the other hand, it does highlight the opportunity to successfully compete (even with GE) and grow within protected market niches.

Product differentiation is a significant contributor to growing the business by increasing market share. It can be engineered into the product, as in the case of quality; but it is often created by adding sales support and service to the product or service offered.

Increased Control over the Channels of Distribution. Approximately 75 percent of the profits associated with the manufacture, distribution, and retailing of foreign-manufactured videocassette recorders are made in this country. Surprised? While Japanese and Korean companies manufacture VCRs for export to this country, distributors and retailers in the United States make 75 percent of all profit associated with those VCRs. Would Sony, Matsushita, and others be interested in integrating forward by acquiring the channels of distribution in the United States? The next several years may see developments in this direction.

Through merger, acquisition, licensing, or franchising, a firm can own a greater portion of the value-added chain through which a product or service progresses. With such growth, more of the profits and more of the market/customer intelligence associated with the product or service go directly to the forward-integrated business. Opportunities in this area are significant. And because quality and service are increasingly important to consumers today, forward integration in some industries is both effective at protecting brand loyalty and profitable.

Increased Control over Suppliers. Sometimes referred to as backward integration, acquiring or merging with suppliers may present growth opportunities if suppliers retain too much of the profits in the value-added chain of the product or service. Because of the CEO's knowledge of the business and of the costs associated with it, he or she may be the first to be alerted to the fact that profits are staying with suppliers. Acquiring or merging with a supplier may also present opportunities to learn more about competitors, to become a lower-total cost producer, and to give a product or service a particular twist that differentiates it from the competitors'.

A caution is in order, however. Gaining control over suppliers has had very mixed results. Analysis of the performance of businesses growing in this fashion reveals that this growth opportunity is often ineffective. The economic benefits foreseen in the business combination are seldom there, notwithstanding all the talk about synergy that often takes place between sellers and buyers.

Acquisition of or Merger with Competitors. In many businesses, a reduction in the number of competitors is very healthy for profit margins. Of course, in some large industries this would lead to monopolistic power and reduce competition to such an extent that the Federal Trade Commission would choose to intervene. But this is seldom the case for companies the size of most entrepreneurial and closely held businesses.

The impact of this growth opportunity, often referred to as horizontal integration, on the profitability of a business can be phenomenal. Improved profit margins often create capital that can be reinvested in some of the other growth opportunities.

Licensing, Franchising, and Cloning. The Benetton family of Italy, best known for colorful sweaters and sportswear that every teenager wants, recognized the power of franchising and worldwide distribution in growing a business. The Benetton siblings, close in age and style preference to their customers (their ages ranged from twenty-two to thirty when they opened their first plant), believed that youth worldwide would want their product, and they had ample market research to back them up. If Benetton did not supply the demand, they knew that others would copy their idea and derive its benefits.

Franchising enabled this young and financially constrained business to exploit explosive growth opportunities. Now, more than twenty years later, it has over 3,000 stores in over fifty countries and opens a new store somewhere in the world every day. Benetton could have simply manufactured the sportswear and exported it, but because it saw greater profit and growth potential in having control over the channels of distribution, it also became a retailer. The fact that financial and risk-management considerations spanned so many national boundaries made franchising a very attractive mechanism for growth.

Licensing a product for overseas manufacture can also generate business for a firm that is not managerially capable of controlling enterprises in different social, cultural, political, and economic environments. Relinquishing control of the product's technology limits the amount of information available to the firm from customer applications as feedback. While not very supportive of continued long-term growth, then, licensing can provide short-term funds at minimum risk and thus aid in the redeployment of financial assets to support a new growth opportunity.

Some businesses are able to recognize the common success factors in the growth and success they have enjoyed so far, and they then clone these factors into new ventures they promote. These clone ventures may be born out of acquisitions, mergers, or internal development.

The Limited, a women's apparel retail chain, has exhibited tremendous growth in the last twelve years. It has gone from $40 million in sales in 1974 to $3.2 billion in sales during 1986 ("The Limited's Unlimited Growth," 1986, p. 98). Leslie Wexner, CEO of The Limited, attributes this success to the company's ability to clone its stores—that is, deploy its management expertise in a standard fashion throughout all of its retail operations. This has been a particular boon in the acquisition and turnaround of other troubled retailers. The Limited now has a consistent operating strategy across its Limited, Victoria's Secret, and Lerner Stores; it cloned the original Limited system in the other operations. Besides replicating procedures and systems, it transfers skilled managers across stores; they act as "carriers" of the proven, "clone-able" ways.

Diversification Thrust

The emphasis in a diversification thrust is on new growth opportunities either in related industries or in totally unrelated ones. Diversification may rely on technical expertise, marketing expertise, the strength of financial resources, or investment expertise. Focusing almost exclusively on entirely new territory, it is the most aggressive growth opportunity. Diversification is more dependent than the holding/maintenance and specialization thrusts on capital and on management capability to manage a diversity of businesses. As a result, information and financial systems and the management of human resources assume primary importance in the implementation of a diversification thrust.

Technology-Based Diversification. Accumulated knowledge and experience in an area of technology can be successfully leveraged by introducing substantially improved products into new markets. (Ideally, of course, these would replace established products in the targeted markets.) The Detroit bottle manufacturer discussed earlier did this when it approached K-Mart with plastic plant-misters. It had an edge—experience in manufacturing plastic bottles for bottlers and distributors—but had never gone directly to retailers and knew little about that market when first making this move.

Market-Based Diversification. A midwestern company has been supplying hospitals with X-ray equipment for the last twenty-five years. Sales growth in this area has slowed in that time, but the advent of medical diagnostics that make use of computer hardware and software has opened new opportunities. Hospital procurement personnel and even heart specialists familiar with the company's CEO are asking him to supply them the new technology. After all, the company already understands their customers' needs and provides reliable service. This is a tremendous growth opportunity— one that rewards years of painstaking care and service of a particular market niche.

Three generations of the Murphy family (name changed to maintain confidentiality) have grown their family-owned business that way. Theirs has been a slow, steady growth through service and knowledge of their customers.

Unrelated Diversification. Many conglomerateurs, both large and small, exploited this growth opportunity during the 1960s and early 1970s. The practice has since fallen into disfavor, however, because the financial performance of acquired and merged companies in areas unrelated to the core business is often dismal. If either the technology or market is unfamiliar—worse yet, if both are— there seems to be little reason to become a conglomerate. But this overlooks the significant growth opportunities available to firms operating in currently unattractive, unprofitable areas. For firms that have the capital and managerial talent to tackle acquisitions or joint ventures in attractive markets, slow entries that allow for learning the new markets and/or technologies can be rewarding growth opportunities.

Geographical Expansion. Broader geographical distribution of products and services within a market niche presents very attractive opportunities for growth. Even with some regional differences in the U.S. market, and with the possibility of strong regional competitors (who have to be studied carefully), it is the safest way to keep doing what your business does best—but on a larger scale.

Exports also present an attractive avenue for growth for U.S. firms with an already established domestic presence. Acquisition of distributors, production facilities, or competitive businesses abroad may facilitate expanding market opportunities, even though they require additional capital and multicultural managerial expertise.

In family-owned businesses, this growth opportunity can be used to provide task-separation across generations, allowing the succeeding generation the opportunity to behave entrepreneurially. Mars, Inc., discussed more fully in Chapter Ten, used this approach to grow the business between the first and second generations. The founder provided his son with the recipe for the Milky Way candy bar and enough seed capital to start making the candy (renamed the Mars Bar) in the United Kingdom.

Investment Outside the Core Business. Those firms seeking a higher-risk growth opportunity might consider investment outside the core business, although this strategy usually requires consider- able liquid capital. Creating a venture-capital firm within the busi- ness is one way to grow. For example, at S. C. Johnson and Son (to be discussed in Chapter Ten), the top fourth-generation contender for the presidency is running the company's venture-capital firm.

Uncovering and Analyzing Growth Opportunities

Creating a master limited partnership in real estate, leasing, exploration is another way of exploiting investment gi opportunities outside the business. Not as risky as diversification or the operating business, investment outside the business diversifies the estate, lowering the total risk. This is especially important in family-owned businesses with dispersed ownership. But it should be noted that investing excessively outside the operating business could effectively drain resources needed for growth opportunities within that business.

Summary

There are three basic thrusts for growth. The holding/ maintenance thrust represents the least amount of change in pursuit of growth and can lead to growth only if it is used for a short period of time, as a foundation-builder for the next growth leg. Both specialization and diversification are, in the short term, riskier and more demanding of significant change and financial resources. But both are strong medicine against aging and the natural forces of decline.

The fifteen growth opportunities under the three basic growth thrusts discussed are the following:

1. Cost reduction
2. Pruning/retrenching
3. Staying put
4. New products
5. Increased control over channels of distribution
6. Increased control over suppliers
7. Increased market share
8. Acquisition of or merger with competitors
9. Quality or customer-service improvement
10. Licensing, franchising, and cloning
11. Technology-based diversification
12. Market-based diversification
13. Unrelated diversification
14. Geographical expansion
15. Investment outside the business

Only a few of these strategies are likely to be appropriate for any given family business's particular situation. Initially, however, even a few is too many. Because growth is very demanding of financial resources and top-management time, it is important to select a single growth opportunity to fuel the business rebirth. The best way to narrow the field is to sift the few attractive alternatives past the screen of business and family goals. That process is the subject of the next chapter.

5

Matching Growth Options to Business and Family Goals

In Chapter Three the discussion focused on the importance of a clear vision for growth and a family consensus about this vision. Chapter Four then explored fifteen alternative growth opportunities. The firm seeking growth now needs to find a match between those growth opportunities and the business and family goals they have identified (see Figure 5).

The Growth Driver

The constraints on financial and human resources at the crossroads make the search for one optimal growth opportunity essential. While in the longer run (a five-to-ten-year period) more than one related growth opportunity may be affordable in the process of regenerating the business, in this critical period the choice is most often limited to one. Managerial capability, managerial time and attention, and financial resources seldom allow the implementation of multiple growth strategies, except perhaps when these are so closely interrelated that one can be implemented with resources generated by the other. In other words, the success of the first strategy implemented may generate slack resources (time and money) for the implementation of a second, related growth opportunity.

**Figure 5. Regenerating the Business: Matching Growth
Opportunities with Business and Family Goals.**

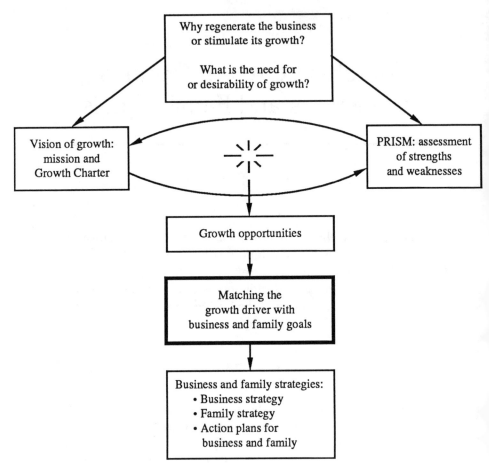

Because the rebirthing effort will be driven by this single growth opportunity, the task is to *choose the growth opportunity that constitutes the best match for both business and family goals and circumstances.* The opportunity chosen is the growth driver.

The following criteria are useful in choosing the growth driver from among competing growth opportunities:

1. The growth driver fits the basic strategy that the business has chosen to pursue.
2. It builds on an established or developing competitive strength.
3. It has not yet been used or fully exploited by competitors; thus it provides the business with a competitive advantage.
4. It is affordable.
5. It is relatively easy to implement, given the firm's unique conditions and the capabilities of management.
6. It does not pose a high risk of deflating employee morale.
7. It does not pose a high risk of creating supplier or customer-relations problems. (These are already "tender spots" in a business at the crossroads.)

Additional criteria for choosing the growth driver from among competing alternatives can be found in Figure 6. The two lists of questions in Table 3 (which break down in detail the *Business Conditions* and *Family Conditions* boxes of Figure 6), will help to screen growth opportunities for business and family considerations simultaneously.

Business Needs and the Growth Driver

Let us take a closer look at some of the questions raised in Figure 6 and Table 3. On the business front, is the growth vision supported by attractive competitive conditions in the particular niche being contemplated for growth? Only a thorough competitive analysis will provide an answer to this question. (Excellent resources on that subject are Porter, 1980, and Ward, 1987.) Who owns the voting stock in the business? This is a very important consideration, because of the extent to which concentrated or dispersed ownership will facilitate or hinder consensus and persistence regarding the vision of growth.

There is no one recipe for growth that is appropriate for all closely held businesses. It is important to consider the questions in Figure 6 and assess how much of a departure from the current formula for business success a particular growth option represents. How is the company organized? Experience, or lack thereof, with divisional or geographical business units will make the implemen-

Figure 6. Narrowing the Choices of Growth Opportunities.

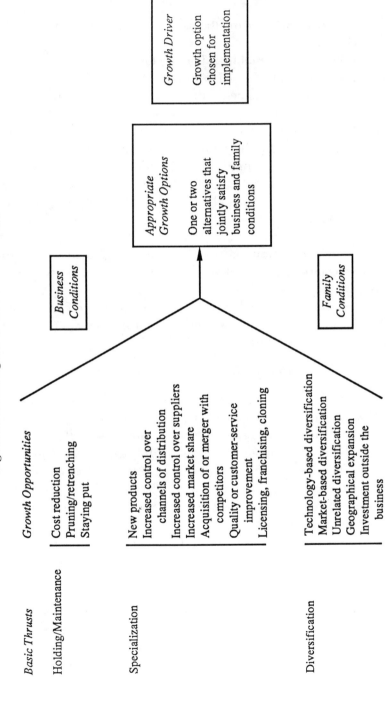

Table 3. Questions About Business and Family Conditions.

Business Conditions

- Does company have a competitively attractive growth vision?
- Is it committed to this vision?
- Who owns the stock?
- Is company organized along divisional, functional, or geographical lines, or centralized?
- How many family members are active in operations/management?
- Does company have capable successors?
- Are capable nonfamily managers willing to work with the next generation?
- Is industry currently attractive and profitable?
- Does company enjoy relative strengths vis-à-vis the competition? What are they?
- Does company have untapped market expertise?
- Does company have untapped technical expertise?
- Does company have the financial resources to support new ventures? To what extent?

Family Conditions

- Is family committed to company's future?
- Is it committed to family unity?
- Can family/business assure founding parents' financial security?
- Can family assure founding parents a fulfilling retirement?
- Does it have capable successors to family emotional leadership?
- How much business education exists among family members?
- Does family have an agreeable estate plan?
- Can it differentiate family membership from business contribution, and sweat equity from blood equity?
- Does it have conflict-resolution skills and mechanisms?
- Is it committed to employees and community?
- Does it have resources to support new ventures by family members?

tation of some growth options easier than others. For example, attempting to grow by controlling channels of distribution without much experience in managing a geographically dispersed organization is a very demanding undertaking. Does the firm have untapped strengths? If it has untapped marketing or technical expertise, for example, a growth opportunity that banks on these may be a comparatively sound way to grow. What are the firm's financial resources? With the possible exception of franchising, licensing, and the holding/maintenance strategies, all growth opportunities require reinvestment in the business. (Figure 7 provides a comparative assessment of the funds required by each of the fifteen growth opportunities discussed.)

Quickly identifying and selecting specific growth opportunities is essential. While the Growth Charter (see Chapter Eight) communicates intention and direction, action to implement appropriate growth opportunities communicates commitment and confidence—essential ingredients of a business regeneration.

Because the risk of any planning activity is that it can become an end in itself, it is important to emphasize that identifying specific growth opportunities that meet family and business goals should never eclipse the importance of customers and attractive markets and market niches. These must remain the backbone of the search for growth opportunities.

How does a business lose sight of the customer in planning for growth? There are two predominant orientations to growing a business. In the first, growth is driven primarily by financial considerations. With this orientation, a business's growth goals are financial objectives to be met. The firm makes operating decisions that seek to optimize internal factors in the accomplishment of these objectives. Company X, for example, decides to build more Product A's than Product B's because the availability of particular raw materials and parts enables the firm to make more money off of A. (In business schools, this exercise is called linear optimization. A wide array of software packages now make the pursuit of such "best solutions" quite feasible to anybody owning a personal computer. As increasing numbers of businesses make use of computer-aided linear optimization, the risk of pursuing growth motivated by financial considerations has increased.)

The risk associated with the financial orientation lies in the sometimes implicit assumption that a market exists for whatever production mix the business sees as profitable at any one time. This inward orientation to business deemphasizes customers, underestimates competitors, fosters the creation of layers of analysts and bureaucrats, and often leads to decline rather than to growth.

The second growth orientation is customer-driven. In contrast, it promotes the creation of a "free-market" culture in the business—one that values customers, respects and worries about the competition, promotes commitment by its employees, and inno-

Basic Thrusts and Growth Opportunities	New Technical Knowledge Required	New Market Knowledge Required	Industry or Market Niche Attractiveness	Funds Required	Commitment to Vision Required
Holding/Maintenance					
Cost reduction	L	L	L	—	L
Pruning/retrenching	L	L	L	—	L
Staying put	L	L	L	—	L
Specialization					
Quality or customer-service improvement	M	L	H	$	M
New products	H	H	H	$	M
Increased control over channels of distribution	M	H	H	$$	H
Increased control over suppliers	H	M	H	$$$	H
Increased market share	L	M	H	$$	M
Licensing, franchising, cloning	H[a]	H[b]	H	$[c]	—
Acquisition of or merger with competitors	L	L	M	$$	M
Diversification					
Technology-based diversification	H	M	H	$$	H
Market-based diversification	M	H	H	$$	H
Unrelated diversification	H	H	H	$$$	H
Geographical expansion	L	H	H	$$	M
Investment outside the business	L	L	H	$$	L
Your own business's growth profile	Current level of technical knowledge [ ]	Current level of market knowledge [ ]	Attractiveness of the industry or market niche represented by growth option [ ]	Funds available [ ]	Degree of commitment present [ ]

Note: L = low, M = medium, H = high.

[a]High for licensing, low for franchising.

[b]High for franchising, low for licensing.

[c]Franchising and licensing are capital generators; cloning is generally *not* capital intensive.

vates both in products/services and in organizational arrangements. This customer-driven orientation nourishes regeneration and growth.

Thinking and acting on growth opportunities both take time. The dilemma of regeneration—particularly if a firm has already begun to decline—is that slack resources, financial and human, may be at a premium. Therefore, the process of identifying and analyzing growth opportunities has to be combined with "growing actions" whose success will create slack resources (money and people) that will enable further planning activity. (See Figure 8.) This interactive process of planning and doing is quite entrepreneurial and appropriate to regenerating the business.

Ideally, this recycling process is of short enough duration that a business can afford to get started. When financial and human resources are constrained at the time the business actively seeks opportunities for growth, the time between development and exploitation must be short. Particularly if decline has already set in, the time between planning and reaping the benefits from growth opportunities is limited.

The interactive and perpetual growing activity portrayed in Figure 9 is captured in the planning-by-doing bias of entrepreneurial experimentation. Cole National, a family-owned business in Cleveland, Ohio, exemplified this bias in its founder's frequent response to his management's proposals on growing opportunities: "So *do* it!" Mr. Cole believed that the only way to conduct R & D in

Figure 8. Planning and Doing in Business Regeneration.

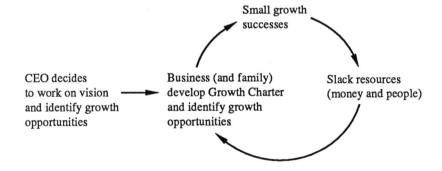

the retail business was to experiment right in the stores. Only by speculating, experimenting, and then regrouping in light of the results could you learn and thus grow the business.

Cole National started in the key distribution business. It gradually grew by leasing and sometimes operating key departments in department stores. Their first retail venture—key shops and outdoor key booths at Sears stores—was quite an attractive value-added service to the retailers. Unlike the competition, which charged the retailer approximately twenty-four cents for a dozen blanks (uncut keys), Cole National charged seventy-five cents for a dozen. For that price, they also included the cutting machine, replacement parts, employee training, miscut key replacements, advertising, employee instruction manuals, and monthly servicing of the cutting equipment—all this at no additional charge to the retailer. Their competitors, on the other hand, provided an employee instruction manual but charged extra for all equipment and additional services. Other retailers who, like Sears, wanted to offer keys to their customers but did not particularly want to be in the key business, breathed a sigh of relief and bought from the value-added service company, Cole National. Cole then reinvested its profitable margins in things other than its merchandise: it invested disproportionately in training employees—both their own and retailers'.

Cole's success in this business led it to clone the retail concept in a variety of high SKU (stock-keeping unit) businesses— eyeglasses, greeting cards, engraving, and others.

Cole National was doing $50 million in sales at an 80 percent gross profit in 1969, twenty-five years after its startup, without a budget or formal strategic plan. It was only in late 1969 that financial plans were developed.

Defining the Core Business

The company's mission statement often provides clues as to what constitutes the core of the business. Is it construction? Or is it real estate development? Or is it the development, construction, and management of commercial real estate? But even further honing of the business core is probably necessary, especially if the business is involved in various product lines, geographical areas, services, or even industries. Two additional questions may further refine the answer: What is the business's reason for being? What does it absolutely *have* to do in order to survive?

Management's familiarity with the technology and the market involved not only helps establish the preliminary definition of the core business; it also helps more precisely define it. Knowledge and expertise in both technology (product and processing technology) and the market determine—and are prerequisites of—the core of your business. In other words, at the heart of your business is knowledge, expertise, and experience with a set of products/services/technologies and a set of customers that allow the business to meet a need in some precise market or market niche.

What is the product/service/technology? What is the market or market niche (that is, who is the customer)? On the basis of those answers, what constitutes the core of the business?

Why is defining the core of the business so important? Much of the process of analyzing growth opportunities hinges on the practicality of each opportunity to the particular business; it hinges, in other words, on the business's managerial capability to capitalize on a particular growth opportunity. The sound way to grow is to do so from the core of the business outward, moving opportunistically but cautiously. The farther afield the growth opportunity lies from the knowledge and expertise represented by the current core business, the more likely it is that managerial and general human resource capability to exploit the opportunity's potential will be lacking.

This particular technology and market-knowledge profile of a business is the foundation from which a well-conceived business growth strategy develops. Cookie-cutter prescriptions for business strategy have proven disastrous for many businesses—firms that got out of businesses they knew and belonged in and into markets or technologies that were either foreign to them or already crawling with competitors.

Because of the potential for such disasters, a key consideration in determining a good match between a growth opportunity and a particular business is the proximity of the new growth opportunity to the core of the business. What matters most, in other words, is the degree of familiarity within the business with the technology and the market involved in the growth opportunity. Knowledge and expertise in either the technology or the market, or in both, significantly affect the attractiveness of one option over another.

The degree of *market* knowledge and experience can be determined by answering several questions:

1. Does the new product/service overlap a market niche already served by the company? (Is the company moving, for example, from glass to plastic bottles?)
2. Does the company know the business under consideration because it has purchased its materials/supplies from the same supplier for years?
3. Has the market been studied and monitored for years by the business as it considered growth opportunities?

Unless the answer to these questions is positive, familiarity with the market does not exist, with two exceptions: somebody in the business may have had experience in that market with another company, or the company may have access to a consultant or market reseracher who knows that market. While these external sources of knowledge may help, they do not represent organizationwide expertise. They may or may not be widespread enough to constitute a market-knowledge advantage.

In focusing on knowledge and experience with the *technology* involved (*technology* is used in its broadest sense, as a system or set of proven practices in retailing, distribution, or manufacturing), management can ask several questions to help determine the advisability of exploiting particular growth opportunities:

1. Does the technology of the new product/service directly overlap technical knowledge required in manufacturing existing products or contained in the current service offered (as was the case, for example, when Cole National grew from key-cutting shops to prescription eyeglass outlets)?
2. Does the business have technical expertise in-house or at a lab or plant that, while not currently used in an existing product,

could be tapped for the new product/service? (Both product technology and manufacturing process expertise are relevant here.)

3. Has the technology been studied and monitored for years by the business as it considered growth opportunities?

Again, reliable advice may be available to the company through an employee's experience with another firm or through consultants or independent laboratories, but such sources do not often translate into meaningful organizationwide familiarity with the technology. If technical knowledge and experience are lacking, other growth opportunities are preferable.

If neither technology nor market familiarity with the new product/service opportunity under consideration currently exists in the business, it is not a viable growth opportunity. The business should not acquire, merge with, joint-venture in, or otherwise attempt to grow into the proposed new opportunity. So-called learning acquisitions and window-on-technology joint ventures are very expensive and should be undertaken only by those whose survival in their current dominant market niche is at stake.

Matching Culture, Capital, and Competence

The culture of the firm and the culture of the family, in addition to familiarity with the technology and market growth, influence the growth opportunity match. Even in acquisitions being made by comparatively "soft-cultured" *Fortune* 100 companies (in contrast to most entrepreneurial and family-owned businesses, which are well known for their strong organizational cultures), greater attention is now being paid to cultural affinity between merging partners and between new ventures and an existing business. While acquisitions and new ventures are usually sought because they offer something different (and ideally complementary) that would create added value for the business, there has to be enough in common culturally for the marriage to work.

Capitalization—that is, the availability of slack financial resources to be invested in new growth opportunities—is also a key consideration in determining optimum growth options. Mergers and acquisitions are nearly always expensive, but their rather immediate value to one's business as a going concern may be extraordinary. Joint ventures can be equally expensive. Both of these approaches may require cost-reduction or retrenchment programs to pay for growth opportunities. Cloning, on the other hand, is often less capital-intensive, either because troubled turn-around businesses are being acquired or because managerial resources need not be expended on developing new procedures and systems; those that are already tried and trustworthy can be adopted. Licensing and franchising can actually be capital-generators in short order.

The unique competence of the CEO and other top management should also play a significant part in a firm's choice of one growth opportunity over another. The ability of owners and top management to exploit growth opportunities is highly related to their knowledge and experience in the market and technology. But knowledge and expertise in planning, organizational development, and transition management are also relevant competencies. Unless management and involved family members have the managerial skills to support growth, significant investment in developing those skills should be made. Many growth horror stories have more to do with the absence of managerial competence in strategic planning and growth management than anything else.

Because of the significant demands on capital for reinvestment, financial management is also a critical area for management in growing businesses. Good business schools can be a resource, providing relevant courses and recommending bright alumni. People and money are always in short supply in firms stimulating business growth; thus both require special attention.

Growth Opportunities and the Family

How committed the owning family is to the revitalization and future growth of the business is a key factor in selecting a vehicle for growth. Is the family solidly committed to growth (or at least supportive of it because of a commitment to family unity)? If so, higher-aspiration growth opportunities such as market-based diversification can be pursued. Otherwise, smaller growth steps such as licensing or franchising may be more appropriate. What about the financial security of the current CEO's generation? If they are financially strapped, their commitment to growth is likely to be weak.

Assuming that commitment is present, is there anybody in the *next* generation who will assume the responsibility for becoming the "glue" of the family during that generation's tenure? If not, family unity may not be much of a foundation on which to build a strategic consensus for growth. Is one next-generation family member more interested in and capable of running the firm than the others? And is the family capable of concentrating owner-ship in one member of the next generation—and thereby focusing leadership—while addressing its desires to be equitable? If owners are unwilling to address estate distribution issues with assets other than the company's stock, less aggressive growth opportunities may need to be pursued. (The less aggressive growth opportunities, as mentioned in Chapter Four, are generally those within the holding/maintenance or specialization thrusts.) Why pursue less aggressive growth opportunities? Because, for example, three one-third-owner siblings can seldom move with the nimbleness and sure-footedness of a single entrepreneur.

Families are very different. Those who believe that only the oldest son should be entrusted with the future of the company usually inculcate this expectation in siblings early in life. They may even concentrate ownership on this oldest son at succession time, so as to ensure business continuity. Other families, while vesting the oldest son with the key management position, insist that ownership be shared equally among siblings in the interest of equity.

There are, of course, families who object to gender and birth-order being the determining factors in succession and think about the future of the family business in very different ways. Merit-based families believe that sweat and ability are what builds equity. Therefore, they develop rules that allow family members to enjoy ownership in the business in direct relation to their contribution to it. Some of these firms develop fairly elaborate formulas for distributing stock based on years of service to the business, the degree of success of the business during those years, or salary (with those in higher-salaried, higher-responsibility positions deriving a greater share of the company).

Other families create elaborate buy-sell agreements among siblings, aunts, uncles, cousins, and others to try to ensure that interest and dedication are what counts. The ability to buy out those who want to pursue alternative careers or ventures prunes the family tree. Still other families have set up venture-capital firms or moved the company to employee ownership to ensure continued entrepreneurial activity in the next generation.

The choice of a particular growth option can be very controversial. If a company's market is not very attractive, or its strengths in that particular niche are being eroded, significant changes may be required to facilitate growth. This often calls on the family to resolve the emotionally charged conflicts that arise as family members hold on to different elements of the difficult reality faced by the business.

A service organization in Illinois, for example, built its reputation around a specialized service to medical laboratories. While business in this specialty had declined significantly, earlier-generation family and nonfamily managers alike refused to listen to suggestions that would curtail some of the original services and change the nature of others. History, tradition, identity, and the security those things provide were at stake. The company remained stuck for a number of years. Finally, an astute member of the next generation of family managers seized an opportunity during a top-management planning retreat (affectionately known as their Woods Meeting, because it was held in a beautifully wooded state park). He acknowledged the importance of the original service to the phenomenal growth of the company and then asked participants whether they would choose to enter the same specialty now, with the investment of people and money it required, given current market conditions. Top management—the older generation included—decided it would not. With that realization, the business got unstuck enough to pursue new service offerings that resulted in renewed growth.

Ease of Implementation

Another key consideration in choosing the growth driver appropriate to a particular business and family is its ease of implementation (Figure 9). Table 4 (a detailed look at the two

Figure 9. Creating an Implementation Strategy for Growth.

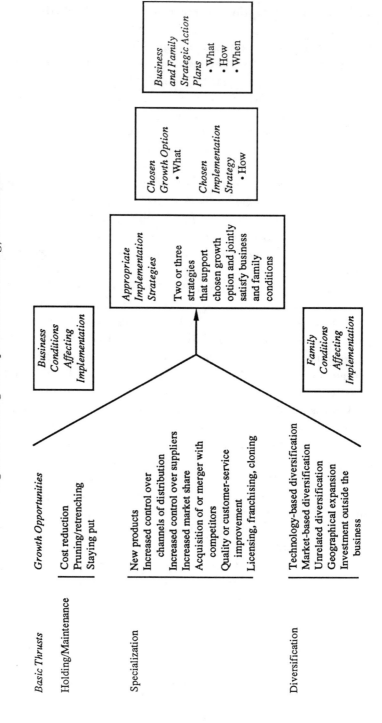

Basic Thrusts

Holding/Maintenance

Specialization

Diversification

Growth Opportunities

Cost reduction
Pruning/retrenching
Staying put

New products
Increased control over
  channels of distribution
Increased control over suppliers
Increased market share
Acquisition of or merger with
  competitors
Quality or customer-service
  improvement
Licensing, franchising, cloning

Technology-based diversification
Market-based diversification
Unrelated diversification
Geographical expansion
Investment outside the
  business

*Business
Conditions
Affecting
Implementation*

*Family
Conditions
Affecting
Implementation*

*Appropriate
Implementation
Strategies*

Two or three
strategies
that support
chosen growth
option and jointly
satisfy business
and family
conditions

*Chosen
Growth Option*
• What

*Chosen
Implementation
Strategy*
• How

*Business
and Family
Strategic Action
Plans*
• What
• How
• When

**Table 4. Questions About Business and Family Conditions
That Affect Implementation of Growth Opportunities.**

Business Conditions Affecting Implementation

- When did the company introduce its last new product?
- What financial resources are available to the company?
- Does company have an ample cadre of highly competent managers?
- Does company have change-management/transition-management skills?
- Does company enjoy brand recognition or superior technology that makes it an attractive licenser, franchiser, or joint-venture partner?
- What would company contribute to an acquired company, other than money?
- Does company have solid manufacturing, engineering, and distribution-logistics expertise?
- Has company accumulated business/products over the years that it would no longer go into, given a choice?
- How attractive/profitable is the industry?
- Is information about business performance widely available throughout the company?

Family Conditions Affecting Implementation

- Is the need for change clear among family members? Do family members perceive *not* changing as a real option?
- Is family committed to company's future?
- What are family communication and interpersonal skills like?
- Do family members have change-management skills?
- Will changes in roles in the business required by growth present role difficulties or feelings of inequity in family?
- What financial resources can be committed to implementing growth options?
- Have steps been taken to provide some liquidity of the estate?

center boxes in Figure 9) lists questions pertaining first to the business and then to family conditions influencing relative ease of implementation of particular growth opportunities by particular businesses and owning families. The core business and the core competencies it creates in the business are at the heart of determining what will be easier for a particular business to implement. If the business has not had any experience introducing a new product in the last twenty-five years—since startup, for instance—the new-product growth opportunity is not likely to be easy. But if the new product is a very attractive opportunity on the basis of other criteria, the solution is not to avoid this opportunity but rather to leverage it by bringing in new-product introduction capability. Hiring consultants, educators, or product managers from a firm that is highly capable in this area is one way of doing this.

The same can be said of strategic planning and management-of-change skills. If the capability does not exist internally, the firm must secure it in some way. Otherwise, implementation is going to be both difficult and deficient.

The Optimum Model

The process of assessing one's business situation should result in a growth profile that provides a strong clue about which growth opportunity constitutes a good match with the business's goals and competencies and is therefore an appropriate growth driver for the business. Figure 7 contrasts the requirements of all fifteen growth options to aid in the assessment of their fit to particular business and family circumstances.

Depending on the growth driver selected, the implementation strategy will include raising cash through the sale of assets and nonperforming product lines, purchasing new plant and equipment, negotiating new marketing arrangements, setting up a subsidiary overseas, establishing new lines of credit to finance the growth, and so on. Both the *what* (which growth opportunity has been selected as the growth driver) and the *how* (implementation strategy) of the particular growth driver should now be clear, and the chosen growth opportunity should have passed through the fit and ease-of-implementation screens captured in Figures 6, 7, and 9.

Summary

Assessing the appropriateness for the business and the family of several growth opportunities at a particular point in time is a prerequisite for growth. Revitalizing the business can be both the cause and the effect of revitalizing the family's commitment to the business. In other words, revitalizing actions in the business often stir owning families into recommitting themselves to a business that may have previously lain moribund. At the same time, managerial actions aimed at regenerating the business depend for their success on the owning family's commitment. Working on getting sufficient commitment to start the regeneration, and then earning the rest based on positive rejuvenating action, is therefore the name of the game.

Growth opportunities have to be screened through the goals and particular conditions of the business and the owning family in order for management to arrive at a match that best drives the growth effort. The constraints on financial and human resources at the crossroads make the search for one optimal growth opportunity, the growth driver, essential.

The growth driver must do the following:

- Fit the basic strategy of the firm.
- Build on established competitive strengths.
- Be affordable.
- Be relatively easy to implement for the particular business and family.

The three basic growth thrusts and fifteen growth opportunities discussed in earlier chapters constitute the universe of regeneration options. A business's particular knowledge and financial profile will determine which growth option is best suited for its regeneration. The risk of any planning activity is that it may lead to paralysis rather than rejuvenating action. Quickly identifying and selecting a specific growth opportunity is therefore important.

Defining the core business is essential to minimizing the risk of all growth choices. At the heart of any successful business is knowledge, expertise, and experience with a set of products/services/technologies and a set of customers—experience that allows the business to meet a particular set of needs in the marketplace. The farther afield the growth opportunity lies from the knowledge and expertise represented by the current core business, the more likely it is that managerial and human resource capabilty to exploit the opportunity's potential will be lacking.

Because of the significant demands on capital for reinvestment posed by growth and regeneration efforts, sound financial management is critical to successfully growing a business. Because degree of family unity and family commitment to the growth agenda will impact strategic and financial considerations, a growth agenda needs to include both business and family recommitment efforts.

Ease of implementation is another major consideration in choosing the appropriate growth driver. The most important issue affecting ease of implementation on both the business and the family fronts is the degree of agreement and clarity about the need to change. If not changing and not growing are seen as viable options, resistance to change is likely to rear its ugly head at implementation time. A sense of urgency for growth and an attractive vision of the future will significantly lower implementation hurdles.

With the growth driver in hand, a strategy and a set of action plans become the blueprint for the regeneration of the business. Those are the subjects of the next several chapters.

6

Developing a Growth Strategy and Building Commitment

Many of the most critical decisions for growth have already been made: the business at the crossroads has made a commitment to growth, brainstormed about growth opportunities, and screened those opportunities to obtain the best match with both business and family circumstances. Focusing all this exploration in a growth strategy, the next step, is simply a matter of setting objectives and making plans to achieve the results intended, while conserving the limited human and financial resources of the corporation. This step also requires staying attentive to the customer and to changing market conditions, for the process of making strategy is a process of continued shaping and crafting—a process that is both intentional and serendipitous.

This chapter is not about strategy as a grand analytical exercise. It is rather about strategy as the culmination of the process of vision creation and about the involvement of owners and others in the business in this vision. It is about crafting a strategy from the accumulated wisdom of the current generation of owners and managers, from the dreams and aspirations of the next generation, and from the emergent wisdom of being loyal to one's customers. It is about arriving at plans that are not validated exclusively by financial analysis or market research data but also by experience, wisdom, and involvement in the details of the business. This is an important chapter, because the development of a strategy for the business is the single best contributor to a sense of direction as well as to cohesion or alignment with this direction within the firm, and both direction and alignment have been shown to be significant contributors to profitability.

Strategy is often associated with change and radical redirection. And yes, radical departures—even revolutions—are unavoidable in some businesses. If change has been resisted or avoided altogether and serious decline has set in, the two-minute warning may have already been sounded. In such circumstances, a strategic redirection may indeed look only to the future for guidance. But that is not the case in most businesses facing the need for rebirth. Generally, the past is a strong contributor to the focused direction emerging for the future. Long-term research done on the strategic activity of firms in the supermarket, automotive, publishing, airline, and garment industries (Mintzberg, 1987) has shown that successful firms *live* strategy in the future but actively *shape* it by learning from the strategic actions of the past. Reflection on patterns of the past result in a profile of capability and potential that then becomes the foundation for growth. Reflection, and actions taken from it—not revolution—is the source of most business growth across generations.

Building the Future on the Past

In earlier chapters, our focus was on vision and growth opportunities—the future of the business. The emphasis here will be different: *respect the past and learn from it what capabilities can propel the business into its desired future. This, in combination with the Growth Charter (see Chapter Eight), is the essence of a workable strategy for the business.*

This orientation to strategy is particularly difficult for management successors, especially the ambitious and very self-confident ones, because it demands an appreciation for both *change* and *stability*. It values what has worked at least as much as what *may* work. And unless the case is well made for the need to promote change and regeneration, the strategy that evolves may well argue for staying the course. Strategy will mean change only if the need for a regeneration has been well established. Only then will seeking growth opportunities be timely; only then will a growing consensus for change be capable of overcoming the natural resistance to it.

Not long ago, a successor in a family-owned business approached me at the end of a strategy seminar and said that it was his father who needed to hear my comments. It turns out that this young man, fresh from a top-notch business school, had tried to install a strategic plan at his father's business. (*Install*, it turns out, is a good description of his attempt.) After months of data gathering, number crunching, and what the son considered brilliant analysis, the strategic plan had been placed on the shelf, never to be looked at again. The father and other key managers considered it insulting and a terrible waste of time.

In his review of some of the firm's operations and departments, the young man had discovered questionable assumptions, a lack of reliable information, and even misdirected efforts; and data from customers pointed to less-than-satisfactory competitive action by the company's sales force. The future successor felt that it was time to confront all these problems and inefficiencies, reshape the company, and redirect its efforts into new areas that he was personally very interested in. Because the report had been shelved, the successor started to get on his soapbox during management meetings. After several months of anger and abrasive behavior toward others, however, he gave up and settled down to business as usual. His energies were now focused on his next move, which he planned to make outside the company.

I asked the young man what he had determined to be the competitive strengths of the company. Without any appreciation for their importance, it seemed to me, he mentioned the quality of the firm's single product and "pretty good" customer service. But he was furious about the terrible waste, the unexploited opportunities in that same market for new products. What he was doing, without realizing it, was questioning the commitment of the owner and key managers that had brought the firm this far. Worse yet, the way he was doing it was undermining others' perceptions of *his* commitment to the future of the business. Strategic planning was becoming the wedge between rather than the bridge across generations of management.

I suggested that when he got back he should ask his father to give him a real job—a job making things and managing people—or that he go to work for somebody else in order to learn about being a change agent before tackling his father's business. Two or three years later, back in the family business, he might be able to form a business strategy group that included his father and other key managers, involving them from the start in any strategic review aimed at redirecting or rebirthing the business. The shame in his case is that the business was indeed in need of a rebirth, but it would not budge without recognition of its own strengths and capabilities for handling future challenges.

It is seldom sheer luck that keeps a business alive for twenty or twenty-five years. And while the experience and accumulated wisdom of the earlier generation may have run their course (meaning that they have become less relevant in a changing marketplace), they still inform those interested in creating the desired future. The patterns of successful and unsuccessful past decisions and actions highlight the capabilities and resources available in the business, just as the color, texture, and hardness of the wood inform the woodworker about creative possibilities.

As an early step in strategy making, the firm needs to identify factors that have helped it get and keep business in the face of competition in the area or even around the world. Exhibit 1 is a potential tool for that identification.

Competitive Analysis

A company's strengths are most meaningful when measured against the competition. For example, a 94 percent on-time record is more likely to be considered a strong competitive advantage if the competition's record is way below this (say 80 percent) and the customer places a high value on on-time deliveries. Thus, a competitive analysis is the next step in the strategy-making process.

Competitive advantages are always determined from the standpoint of customers, of course; they are the benefits the customer *perceives* in buying from Company A as opposed to buying from a competitor. Having the low-cost position, for example, is not a competitive advantage unless the business uses

Exhibit 1. Competitive Strengths Checklist.

	Strong relative to competition? Check if yes.	Value to the customer: high, medium, or low.
Lack of competition?		
Price?		
Price/performance (that is, value)?		
Quality?		
Customer service?		
Reliability?		
On-time delivery record?		
Product customization?		
Inventory/product availability?		
Product line breadth?		
Personal relationships with customers?		
Personal relationships with suppliers?		
Industry association membership?		
Trained workforce?		
Geographical proximity?		
Access to raw materials?		
Access to inexpensive energy?		
Access to capital?		
Low transportation costs?		
Technology employed?		
Credit arrangements for customers?		
Channels of distribution?		
Other?		

this strength to carry out a low-price marketing strategy and customers are price-sensitive.

Competitive analysis should include an appraisal of the current strategies of competitors, the markets they serve, the degree to which they are satisfying customer needs, the major product/service lines offered, and the technologies used. A good competitive analysis should also include a review of the major functional policies of the relevant competitors. What, for example, is Competitor Y's marketing policy? Is it niche or mass marketing? Aggressive pricing to build market share or healthy profit margin maintenance? Functional policies in human resources, finance, manufacturing, and other areas should also be reviewed.

Next a competitive analysis should, on the basis of observed competitive behavior, spell out the objectives of competitors and their degree of commitment to those objectives. If the objective of a firm is cash flow and the owning family is growing and shows no signs of wanting to reinvest in the business, that competitor may be highly committed to its objective to the exclusion of a series of available competitive moves. That leaves the field clear. The real test then becomes the extent to which current management is willing to stretch out to ways of competing that are not an established strength for the company, and the extent to which the agents of change in the next generation are willing to fully capitalize on any stretching out. On the other hand, it is as foolhardy for a firm to venture without adequate planning and preparation into a product, service, or market where no strength or capability has traditionally existed as to stand still for fear of the risk of growing.

Finally, competitive analysis should include any recent moves or announcements by the competition. Did Competitor Z just announce a joint venture with Company X? What impact could this have on the business? This information, along with some appraisal of the environment (economy, government regulations, demographic trends, and so on) and plenty of self-analysis, should then lead to a well-grounded set of strategy options.

In general, good prescriptions for entrepreneurial and closely held businesses are strategies that rely on product customization, customer service, product quality, personal relationships, and industry and community involvement. The element common to all of these strategies is the recognition that tackling market segments or niches, rather than entire markets, can be quite profitable and growthful. Indeed, such strategies lead to much more balanced growth and higher returns on assets than the traditional overriding concern of large public corporations to grow market share at all costs in large markets.

Entrepreneurial and closely held businesses compete best in segments or niches where their own strengths are most highly valued by customers, which means that these strengths result in an important and sustainable competitive advantage. These businesses also use R & D to reduce manufacturing costs and improve product performance even through recessionary periods, thereby improving value to the customer; and they continue to invest in advertising and the training and development of people through the lean years. This long-term orientation is common to strategies pursued by entrepreneurial and family-owned businesses.

Obstacles to Strategy Implementation

The most often encountered obstacles to successful implementation of new strategies have more to do with managerial capability, or its absence, than with any other factor. For example, problems with or complete failure of strategies are often attributed to deficient market analysis, inadequate planning skills, or an underestimation of the competition, the capital needs, or the effort needed to launch the new growthful venture. Management focus on the short-term "fire-fighting" bias and its inability to clearly communicate the need for change are also frequently cited as obstacles. Yet all of these obstacles could have been removed or minimized by a concerted educational effort aimed at both managers and owners.

The formulation of strategy is not something to be done by strategic planners or consultants but rather by CEOs and top-line management. But in order for management to plan and implement strategy successfully, managerial capability in "strategic thinking" often needs to be increased. Professional consultants, business school programs, and trade associations can help on this front.

Other obstacles often mentioned are the cost of strategy

implementation, customer dissatisfaction as a result of the confusion or shifting emphasis created by a period of change in strategies, and a lack of real management commitment to the new strategy.

Several factors affect ease of implementation regardless of which growth opportunity is chosen. The most important of these on the family front is the degree of family unanimity about the need to change. *If not changing is perceived as a viable choice, it is very likely that resistance and lack of commitment will rear their ugly heads at implementation time.* Why? Because while talking of change and envisioning its consequences may be difficult, actually changing the way things are done is usually disruptive and painful. In the short term changes represent a real loss, be it financial (lower dividends) or emotional (more work and stress). The implementation stage makes the cost of changing very real indeed.

Therefore, change-management skills at the business and family levels are an important capability, as are communication and problem-solving skills—and the discipline to allot time for these activities. And of course finances are important. If the business and the family give themselves some breathing room, perhaps by refinancing the business and/or achieving some estate liquidity, implementation is likely to be easier. Big successes will not be required from the new growth opportunity immediately. The less affordable the growth opportunity is to the business and the owners, the higher the probability for implementation difficulties, unless developmental plans such as those just mentioned are put in motion.

Factors that contribute to the ease of implementation of *any* growth opportunity are listed below. If these factors are present in business, family, and employees, the firm has a strong start on the demanding task of regenerating the closely held business.

With Regard to Management

1. Ownership is concentrated in family members who are active in the management of the firm.
2. The company is organized so as to allow family members and key nonfamily managers distinct areas of managerial responsibility and authority. Departments, divisions, regions, or busi-

ness teams provide distinct territories in which to work and excel.

3. A vision of the future and a mission statement exist that address the need for change and growth within the business and the family. These help family members commit to the future of the company.

4. The managerial life cycle of a single generation does not significantly exceed twenty-five years.

5. A board of directors (with active outsiders) meets regularly.

With Regard to Family Members

1. At least one member of the founding or current generation of family provides the emotional "glue" and support that bind the family unit together.

2. There is a tradition of family group activity.

3. Family roles are flexible, and leadership responsibilities are shared.

4. Communication is significant, and information about the business and the family is kept separate (but both kinds of information are widely shared).

5. Problem-solving, conflict resolution, and consensus-reaching skills are present in the family.

6. An active family council or family board meets regularly and secures family needs and interests.

With Regard to Individual Employees of the Company

1. Employees have opportunities over the years to work alongside several members of the owning family.

2. Employees "make a difference" at work, though they are not "family."

3. Employees have opportunities for growth and development.

4. Employees are rewarded for helping the business and the family grow, whether through promotions, a stock plan, or a company bonus.

5. Employees, in time, become members of the extended family— the blood-and-sweat family.

Commitment to the Company Strategy

The strategic management process is a critical tool for the top management of organizations operating in a fast-changing business environment. Businesses continually face the challenge of increasing employee (and family) commitment to the business's strategy. How else will the new strategy be thoroughly and aggressively implemented? How else will the strategy be translated into action at the point of contact with the customer? How else will the strategy result in a sustainable competitive advantage for the organization? In a closely held business, how else will nonmanaging owners support growth opportunities?

The last decade has seen a lot of strategic planning activity. Still, much action by managers and owners alike continues to be aimed at nonstrategic considerations rather than at those basics that give the firm staying power in the competitive arena of the marketplace. Staying power lies in the ability of various departments of a business to work together to integrate resources and successfully implement strategy.

The results of strategic planning have not met expectations; problems are manifold. In companies where a strategic planner is on staff and strategic planning meetings are held, nonmanaging owners often feel left out, so they worry about their dividends. People at lower levels of the organization often complain that they are less in touch with the company direction after strategic planning exercises begin than before. Middle managers, supervisory personnel, and salespeople also report having less influence in the all-critical company-customer contact. They also find themselves less sure of how appropriately they are dealing with the competition. They feel less ownership in the business and its future, which often results in inaction or extreme caution. All of these complaints are symptomatic of strategic planning failing at its most basic level—getting people committed to the future direction of the firm.

When lack of commitment is raised as a problem, managers and owner-operators respond something like this: "A written and widely communicated strategy is no strategy at all." And because secrecy is seen as an asset, managerial actions to address the problem consist, at best, of a strategy-briefing meeting, a day-long owning-family communications retreat, or a colorful brochure describing the new mission or competitive position statement.

But predictability and a lack of commitment—not disclosure—may be the greatest risk to a business's strategy. By relying on standardized analytical formats to arrive at the content of a strategic plan and displaying organizational inertia while conditions in the marketplace change, a company may too clearly reveal its strategy to its competitors through its actions, or lack thereof.

For firms at the crossroads, the process of recommitting to growth and needed change brings very significant benefits, although we ought not minimize the importance of the content and soundness of the strategy chosen. Much discussion and communication among family members and employees is needed for this recommitment to take place.

The Family Business Commitment Plan

Having chosen the growth driver optimal for both business and family, family members must now put down in writing the nature of their commitment to the future of the enterprise. This commitment plan is meant to answer the question, *What do we have to do to ensure the future health and growth of the business?* A paragraph or two, along with a record of appropriate commitment-building action steps, is all that is necessary. Before moving on, the firm must assess whether decisions about a growth option are based on careful analysis of business strengths and weaknesses and the market's threats and opportunities. Other factors that have little to do with the competitive reality of the business or the honest assessment of owning-family considerations conspire in favor of overcautiousness and conservatism. If there is little confidence in the next generation, is it due to a lack of information or to a knowledge of shortcomings? Is there uncertainty about family members' preferences to work either together under one roof or within a multidivisional structure? Such factors should not be left unresolved: lack of confidence in the future of the economy may be significant, and not knowing the degree of corporate commitment present among members of the next generation can seriously undermine the objective assessment of a viable growth strategy for the business.

Information needs to replace uncertainty. Communication among family members—between spouses, across generations, between siblings and uncles and aunts and cousins—needs to be promoted and supported. There really is no good substitute for communication. It can take place in informal family gatherings, in meetings facilitated by outside consultants, in therapeutic settings, or better yet in strategy-making meetings at which all are free to talk about dreams, aspirations, and the future of the family business.

Strategy and the Board of Directors. Boards of directors, boards of advisers, "kitchen cabinets," and asset boards are all useful mechanisms for the task of *reviewing strategy and growth plans* for consistency with the Growth Charter, affordability, and fit with the business's competencies and the family's goals and values. *Review* does not mean involvement in developing the strategy but rather advice, oversight, and loyal criticism after the strategy is developed.

Effective board members need the latitude to disagree constructively, so that they can add value to business strategies and plans. They must be smart, business- and industry-knowledgeable, high-achievement people. Board members must also care enough about the business and its owners to speak up when owners underestimate the competition. They should be complementary to and not complimentary of the owners' expertise. They must also alert owners and top managers to key environmental factors (such as regulations, demographic changes, economic growth) affecting the business in the future. "Club members" do not belong on these boards. Club membership rules were a significant factor in the decline and death of the *Saturday Evening Post* and Curtis Publishing. Firms need board members who will do their homework, know the numbers, look beyond the numbers, and ask the right questions (not just the comfortable ones).

Research by John Ward (1986) suggests that family-owned businesses tend to undershoot or be less aggressive about their strategies than a good strategic analysis would prescribe. Outside board directors can be highly influential in raising the expectations and the self-confidence to meet these high expectations in the family-owned firm. Directors also make great role models and perhaps even mentors for the next generation, and they can provide an objectivity that emotion has a tendency to drive out in familial contexts.

Strategy and the Family. Individual differences—be they generational, gender-related, or due to sibling order or business roles—all threaten the viability of family consensus about the future of the business and the family itself. But much of what is condemned as irreconcilable differences, greed, stubbornness, disloyalty, lack of commitment, and even lack of competence in discussions about the future of the family business at the crossroads is only slightly more complicated than a simple failure to communicate. Certainly the *basic* problem is a failure to communicate. A lack of communication is at the root of a failure to educate, to instill the important values of cooperation, and to promote compromise through ongoing dialogue and personal example. It is also behind a failure to create organizations and systems that allow for differences while valuing teamwork and togetherness.

But it is almost never too late to change. In fact, strategy disussions can become a timely excuse for reestablishing connections within the organization—a reason for renewing commitments and recreating the mutual respect and fun shared in earlier times, when life was simpler and the "kids" were much younger. A renewal of communication is not easy, however. Significant investments of time, emotional energy, and money (to bring in consultants, professors, counselors) often have to be made over a period of years. The alternative is to let a crisis bring the family together, although not even a crisis may bring people together with regard to the future, especially if the emotional distance between them is significant.

Owner families have to schedule periodic meetings to talk about the mission of the firm and the family; about vision, strategies, and commitments; and about the next generation, key employees, money, dividends, and the estate. Secrecy is deadly in strategy and in the affairs of the family in business. Ideally, strategy can provide a rationale for more open communication and a more open stance toward a future of opportunities for the next generation.

Perhaps a series of one-day family meetings could be scheduled over the course of a year. These could meet needs for further business education in, for example, product, marketing, finances, ownership, and strategy. Equally important, however, family communication and team-building needs could be granted a part of each day's agenda, as well as some form of family rest and recreation time. (Family R & R does wonders for togetherness and family nurturance.) At the end of this series of meetings, the owning family could very well be ready to align the firm's structure with the growth strategy, the subject discussed in Chapter Seven.

Summary

Strategy is the culmination of the process of vision creation. It is to be crafted out of the accumulated wisdom of the current generation of owners and managers, from the dreams of the next generation, and from the emergent wisdom of loyalty to customers. Development of a strategy is important, because its presence is the single best contributor to both direction and alignment with the chosen direction within the firm, both of which have been shown to be significant contributors to profitability.

Analysis of the patterns of successful and unsuccessful past decisions and actions highlights the capabilities and resources available in the business. These, along with the vision of a desired future contained in the Growth Charter, need to inform the crafting of a business strategy. Competitive advantages, from the perspective of the customer, constitute the foundation for sound growth. A thorough competitive analysis is therefore a must. It needs to include the following:

- An appraisal of the current strategies of competitors, the markets they serve, the product/service lines they offer, and the degree of customer satisfaction they achieve with their product and/or services
- A review of the functional policies of relevant competitors

- A review of competitors' objectives and their commitment to them
- Information about recent competitive moves that may provide clues to a changing competitive strategy
- An appraisal of the overall economic, political, and social environment

Good strategies for entrepreneurial and family-owned businesses often rely on excellent customer service, product/service quality, strong personal relationships, and high industry and community involvement.

The most often encountered obstacle to successful strategy implementation is lack of managerial capability. Concerted educational efforts can make a significant contribution to growth at the crossroads.

Boards of directors, boards of advisers, and family asset boards are all useful mechanisms for the task of reviewing strategy and growth plans. The review needs to be particularly concerned with consistency between the strategy developed and the Growth Charter, with the strategy's affordability, and with the strategy's fit with the business's core competencies and goals and with the family's goals and values.

Owner families should schedule periodic meetings to talk about the mission of the firm and the family; about vision, strategies, and commitments; and about the next generation, key employees, money, dividends, and the estate. Family asset boards and family councils can help overcome the deadliest tendency in the affairs of a family in business: the tendency toward silence and secrecy. Strategy discussions can provide a rationale for more open communications and often result in a healthier family and a more open familial stance toward growth opportunities for the business.

7

Aligning
the Company's Structure
with the Growth Strategy

Businesses require capital, human resources, energy (electricity, gas, and so on), information, and materials. They then combine these in some fashion to produce goods and services that demonstrate added value. In other words, businesses are systems; and like other systems they secure inputs, process them in some particular way, and produce outputs that have added value. The effectiveness of a business is partially determined by the value it adds in converting raw materials into valuable outputs. Significant loss of capital, energy, human effort, or material in the conversion process represents waste, reduced competitive fitness, and a reduction in organizational energy available for growth.

The objective of restructuring the organization in growth-seeking businesses is to increase the yield (or value-added capability) under conditions of strategic change. This is often accomplished by promoting autonomy by product, technology, or geography, so that independent units can operate in a fully competitive, free-market environment. The increased exposure helps businesses retain their competitive fitness and entrepreneurial edge.

In family-owned businesses, restructuring also serves to develop the managerial abilities of successors and helps reduce conflicts between potential successors (often siblings). It may also help reduce the amount of heat generated by friction between the founder and the next generation, so that the light of reason may prevail.

Organizational restructuring encompasses more than mere tinkering with the lines and boxes of a structure. It may include altering the structure or hierachy of the family by, for example, naming the youngest sibling president of the company because of his/her competence and zeal. It also involves the softer, more dynamic side of the organization: the culture of the firm, the capability of its human resources, the problem-solving skills of family and business systems, the communication and information practices followed, and the mechanisms for board review and business regeneration.

The discussion of organizational restructuring will consider boards (of advisers, of directors, and asset boards), alternate equity structures in the business (the use of voting, nonvoting, and preferred stock, for example), and management practices that encourage continued entrepreneurship and stimulate growth across generations of managements and families.

Organizational restructuring also encompasses transition management activities. Because restructuring is the dynamic process of moving an organization from one form to another, the times between business growth spurts are well spent in shaping the organization for continued growth. These may also be opportune times to begin significant changes and transitions in goals, roles, and ways of relating in families that own businesses.

Organizational restructuring is an important element in stimulating business growth, because form has a significant impact on function. Organizational and family structures that are not designed to promote growth will spawn a tremendous waste of human energy and financial resources when allowed to do so. They will lead to the erosion of the will to grow. Researchers have discovered that a lack of fit between the strategy of a business and its structure has significant negative implications for that business's survival and success (Brittain and Freeman, 1986). Equally dramatic is the evidence that entrepreneurial behavior occurs in organizational contexts where bureaucratic and stability-seeking management practices are at a minimum. Entrepreneurial behavior flourishes only in organic and flexible settings, which permit opportunity-seeking actions that result in growth of the business.

A lack of strategy/structure match in family-owned businesses may also contribute negatively to family harmony and the emotional well-being of family members. Family firms are often paralyzed and unable to live up to their potential because the hardware (organizational chart or family hierarchy) and software (roles, power, information, organization, and family culture) of organizational structuring create dysfunctional behavior. This is typically a total system problem, not just the problem of an individual family member, the family, the business, or an individual member of management. This is one reason why many family firms couple changes in the structure of the business with changes, often brought about by crisis, in the family hierarchy (Hershon, 1975).

High-performing businesses need vision and the capability to accomplish that vision without undue hardship. Along with a growth strategy, organizational restructuring (in the total system sense) is a key element in removing obstacles on the road to the vision of growth. Central to its importance is the management of human energy in organizational settings, the major leadership challenge posed by organizations of the 1990s.

A quick diagnostic of potential blocks to this energy was discussed in Chapter Three. By looking at power, roles and responsibilities, information, strategy, and management (PRISM), the leader of an organization can assess the present state or current operating conditions of the business and of the family in the business.

Restructuring: What It Entails

What needs to be done to start moving the total system—the CEO, the business, and the family—in the direction of growth? A leader's actions ought to be concentrated on creating appropriate structures for the business and the family owners (whether involved in management of the business or not), promoting ongoing problem-solving activities, and educating and developing employees and owners. Other key CEO interventions include influencing or fine-tuning the culture of the organization and perhaps the family to fit the decision to rebirth the business, and actively managing the transition or regeneration state within which all this changing for the sake of renewed growth will be done. The CEO should also encourage the board to review the actions being taken (and their results), monitor the sources and uses of capital and the capital structure of the firm, and synchronize all of this with management practices that implement the Growth Charter in the day-to-day operation of the business.

Review the Strategy

After arriving at a strategy for the owners based on appropriate growth opportunities and ways of realizing them, business strategists must then subject it to review. At least one study on successful growth through diversification (Lauenstein, 1985) points to a critical advantage of diversified corporations over specialized competitors. Diversified corporations are structured so that a top-management group actively supervises the performance of specialized companies underneath. Specialized competitors, if they are enlightened, have a board of directors; but these directors seldom see as their responsibility the detailed review and loyal but critical monitoring of the business strategy and other managerial decisions. This is particularly true in entrepreneurial and family-owned businesses, where "foundership" and ownership bestow a high degree of power on the CEO.

Well-managed diversified corporations do not forgive mediocre plans or performance by presidents and general managers of the companies that make them up. In entrepreneurial and family-owned businesses, which have ego, ownership, and blood to consider, forgiveness may indeed be appropriate to the health of the family. But is it conducive to business health? Not always. Active, involved review by outsiders on the board of directors is therefore strongly recommended before a firm embarks on structural changes.

Promote Teamwork

There are several types of organizational structure that have shown themselves capable of promoting growth and handling the complexities that accompany it. One common element to all of them is the team.

There are many kinds of teams. (See Figure 10.) Some combine members from several functional departments—for example, marketing, engineering, and manufacturing. Their mission is often to make the organization more agile in responding to problems created by changing customer or market requirements. They often operate as temporary task forces and are disbanded as soon as a given problem is resolved.

Task, project, product, or service teams—the terms are nearly synonymous—perform a function similar to that of task forces, but they are recognized as a necessary and full-time feature of the organization. Business or business center teams are often given profit-and-loss, return-on-investment, or return-on-assets responsibility. Matrix organzations typically weave several of these teams into the fabric of a functional organizational structure, promoting more teamwork across departments. When these teams are given additional authority and financial responsibility, they may be known as business units or divisions.

The matrix structure recognizes both functional and business or customer teams and promotes a matrix of reporting and review relationships between these two. It is designed for efficiency in the use of often expensive functional expertise—for example, specialists—while aligning these human resources with the particular needs of a customer. The matrix is better able to handle the boom-and-bust cycles inherent in some industries, by allowing easier reassignment of people to different projects. Of course, there are

Figure 10. Team Structures for Growth.

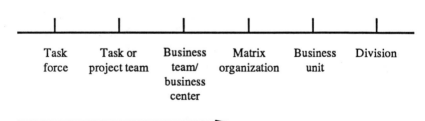

Increasing "teamness" and autonomy to pursue a growth strategy

complications to the double-reporting relationship. And because matrix designs have been extensively used in defense businesses, which are typically overexposed to the bureaucracy of their customers, the matrix has become associated with complexity and bureaucracy, the enemies of growth.

The matrix structure is, at the very least, an effective transitional organization. Regardless of the nature of the business, if it has been organized around traditional functions such as marketing, engineering, and production, it can often use a healthy dose of teamwork in order to grow. The matrix, then, may be an effective structure with which to begin movement in the direction of greater product or business unit responsibility and greater customer orientation. Businesses often shift from the use of matrix structures to business unit or divisional structures within a period of three to five years.

Amax (a fictitious name), a family-owned southern furniture company, has grown to approximately $350 million in sales in its sixty years of existence (and three generations of owner-managers) by structuring itself as a collection of small companies. Its growth has been achieved primarily through acquisitions in exchange for company stock. The company structured each newly acquired business as a separate division with profit-and-loss responsibility. Their guiding principle was that people do their best job when they are closest to running their own business. Yet structural decentralization is only part of Amax's success story. This company has further supported the people-as-owners principle with generous profit-sharing and employee stock purchase plans.

Like matrix structures, the other team structures discussed have a spotty record of success. But the problems are problems of implementation; they are not inherent in the team concept itself. Regardless of which team structure makes most sense in a particular situation, effective teams require the following:

1. *Strong support from upper management in the organization.* This is particularly true of temporary or informal teams, which sooner or later require that the formal/hierarchical organization continue to implement what they have developed. This need gives rise to teams described variously as "umbrella," "support" or "sanctioning" teams; these are often created at least one level above

the task or business team and support it with resources, information, and the running of interference.

2. *Clear statement of team task or mission.* The team needs to be given a clear statement of expected results: what needs to be accomplished and by when. If a newly formed team has to spend a lot of time in meetings, figuring out what it is expected to do, it is off to a bad start. Team members may still need to discuss and develop their mission and goals, but with clear guidelines they have no need to do so in the dark.

3. *Training in team-building and meeting skills.* There are very few "natural" teams around, except during times of crisis, when a clearly visible common problem demands that people team up quite readily. Whole communities, for example, coordinate their efforts in response to the damage of tornadoes, earthquakes, or public transportation strikes. But under normal circumstances, if the business wants a team, it needs to invest, during startup, in providing its members with behavioral science methods that promote good communication skills, effective problem-solving techniques, and strong consensus-reaching capabilities.

4. *A facilitator, process consultant, or meeting coach who continues to promote the learning of the initial team building in regular work meetings of the team.* This role may be performed by a personnel person or an outside consultant, or it may fall on individual team members with a natural ability to do such work.

5. *Rewards and recognition for the work done in the team.* This is again particularly important for teams that are not a formal or permanent feature of the structure. If all the recognition, advancement, and pay increases come from duties done outside of the team structure, the initial commitment of team members is undermined. In Western societies especially, individual recognition and rewards are important elements of good team functioning.

"Lean and mean" or "flat" organizations are often thought to be the most effective, and team structures make leanness possible. Communication, coordination, and resourcing across functions or departments are handled by team members themselves, requiring that less of this be done by middle managers, such as area supervisors, assistant superintendents, and so on. The fewer layers there are between the work that gets done and managerial authority for quality, cost, and customer service, the faster and less distorted management information becomes. This results in more opportunity-seeking behavior and more nimbleness in responding to opportunities in the marketplace—the essence of a growth strategy.

Align the Business and the Family

The structure of the family can also contribute much to growth. For example, in the family-owned business, the structure of the family helps determine whether the joint business-family system is aligned—that is, in the same phase and headed in the same direction. Alignment is a much easier state for the founder, family, and business to be in during the creation/birth and early growth stages of the firm. To a large degree, the overlap between the business and its founder is still nearly complete. (See Figure 11.) All work and no play (since work *is* the play) makes the entrepreneur thrive with high energy.

In the later stages of growth and business maturity, and in the presence of family members of the next generation, alignment is a difficult quality for business and family to maintain. Sibling rivalries, family hierarchies that are inverted in the business (when, for example the younger brother is the CEO and the older brother is

Figure 11. Alignment Between Family and Business During Various Stages of Business Development.

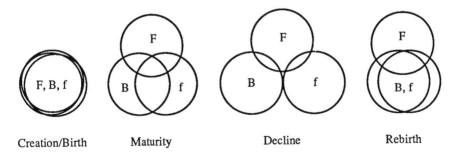

Creation/Birth   Maturity   Decline   Rebirth

Note: F = founder, B = business, f = family.

the vice-president of marketing), and percentage of equity owner-ship unrelated to function in the business may all interfere with alignment. However, changing the family structure and its behavioral patterns may increase alignment between family, business, and the growth strategy.

The elements of family structure include power position in the family, age, gender, role, and (for owners) equity structure. While no one can do much about the age and gender of family members, the assumptions and patterns that accompany those can certainly be altered. Because different family cultures (ethnic differences included) produce different patterns of behavior, altering cultures to make them more functional for the business and the family seeking growth is worth considering.

The power structure is also flexible. Families can do much to change patterns and structures that, for example, concentrate all the authority on the founding entrepreneur. Leisure time, community and industry association work, teaching, and writing are all possible tasks that permit a CEO to reduce the power that comes if he or she is always in command of the ship.

Life cycles of the different generations of the family, when their implications are understood, can be made to work for the benefit of the family and the business. S. C. Johnson and Son, discussed further in Chapter Ten, is working on the succession process at a time in the life cycle when father and sons generally experience less conflict (Davis, 1982). The fourth-generation father is in his late fifties, and fifth-generation family members are in their late twenties. Samuel C. Johnson III (the CEO) has implemented a matrix organization and insists on concentrating equity ownership in the hands of the members of the next generation willing and capable of running the business. He is even willing to split the business into separate entities, giving the next-generation member running each business unit majority ownership. Such is the current CEO's belief in the power of organization and equity structures to alter the course of a business's capacity to survive and grow.

Realign the Capital Structure

The deregulation of the financial industry and the inability of traditional sources of financing to keep pace with demands for

money to fund worthwhile projects have led to an explosion of
financial structures and instruments during the last decade. (Many
of these are discussed in Resource A, "Financing the Costs of
Growing a Business.") The impact on entrepreneurial and family-
owned businesses has been extraordinary. Business equity can be
voting or nonvoting and have many different dividends associated
with it (Class A common, Class B common, and preferred A and B
may all pay different dividends, for example). The corporation can
be structured as a master limited partnership, with the next
generation as general partners of their own business units. The
master partnership units can trade in the public markets and thus
provide the company with growth financing. New debt instruments
also abound. In fact, the financial options are unlimited. In this era
of fierce competition in the financial industry, the borrower is king,
and financing needs are being met in very tailored ways by financial
institutions. When new products or lines of credit are created by
lenders to respond to one customer's needs, the lenders discover an
untapped market. Product innovation allows the borrower to get
money on his or her own terms. And many of these concepts or
products then become replicable through private placements.

What implications do the source of financing and the capital
structure of the firm have for growth? Do some arrangements
stimulate business growth while others stifle it? Do some financing
methods pit the needs of the business against the needs of the family
in a family-owned business? The answer is yes.

Improved cash-flow management, which shortens the cash
cycle of the business, has the least negative impact on the future
discretion of managers and owners. But the amount of capital this
strategy generates may not be sufficient to stimulate a rebirth of the
business.

Debt financing, in its many forms, remains quite favorable
for businesses that want to retain full ownership control. Of course,
large amounts of debt may carry more covenants and restrictions
than other arrangements do. In highly leveraged companies, bankers may want to have a say in inventory levels, quarterly earnings,
and therefore even executive salaries and perks. The discretionary
advantage of debt financing may then disappear.

Venture capital and subsequent rounds of equity financing

are the largest capital-generators for growth. In capital-intensive or fast-growing markets, they are the best source of growth-stimulating capital. Their consequences to the company's capital structure are the following: (1) equity is in the hands of strangers, often with different objectives than the founder's; (2) the board of directors is subject to greater scrutiny and more intense short-term pressures; and (3) a repurchase to make the company private again may become (assuming fast growth and earnings momentum) prohibitively expensive.

Besides, venture capitalists are not interested in families. They back individual entrepreneurs who have visions of growth that do not include the next generation of family members. An entrepreneur with intentions of simultaneously optimizing the growth of the business and the health and growth of the family should be cautious about venture-capital financing. He or she may eventually be forced into a position of sacrificing the family.

Going public is largely an irreversible decision. On the bright side, converting some of the equity into cash via public markets does allow families to diversify their estate. This satisfies individual needs for asset diversification without forcing the company into ill-advised product or market diversification. Financially driven diversification that moves away from the core of the business into something for which a company lacks technology and/or market knowledge can be fatal.

The source of capital largely determines its use and the consequences of such use. Therefore, sources of capital may need to be converted—that is, rolled over—as the leader's vision changes. An entrepreneur whose initial identification with the business was very absorbing and exclusive of the family (the business-as-mistress phenomenon) may come to see, as his or her children become young adults interested in the business, that a regeneration of the business is worth the effort. It may even be worth the complications of going to bankers or the capital markets.

What must CEOs do to stimulate business growth and rekindle the flame of entrepreneurship? They could try to create a common vision that aligns the family around business growth. If the financial requirements of new growth are well understood, dividend policy could be largely determined by the decision to grow.

When the decision to rebirth the business is made, recapitalizing the company by exchanging high-dividend–paying preferred or common stock with lower-yielding common stock, for instance, may be appropriate. Family members need to understand that, in exchange for dividends, they are reinvesting in the business in the hope of being contributors to its continued growth. They will thus derive the satisfaction of contributing to something larger than themselves now and quite possibly obtaining larger capital gains sometime in the future.

Profit sharing and employee ownership also contribute significantly to continued growth and maintenance of the entrepreneurial edge. Amax, the family-owned southern furniture company discussed earlier, has used both techniques to further the growth-stimulating effects of a highly decentralized structure. The family and the employees now own about 35 percent of the outstanding shares.

A study of American Business Conference companies by the consulting firm McKinsey (Clifford and Cavanagh, 1985) revealed that the best-performing companies in this group (measured by sales growth, return on equity, assets, and jobs created) had an average 31 percent of the stock owned by employees themselves. In the larger pool of *Forbes* 100 companies, average employee ownership is only 4 percent.

Profit sharing, employee ownership, and other individual and group-based reward systems encourage continued growth and opportunity-seeking entrepreneurial behavior. Unlike dividends and executive perks that help the business at tax time but will not help stimulate growth, they expand the definition of ownership of the business and therefore stimulate more people to work like owners. But family-owned businesses considering sharing ownership with employees need to be aware that it will require much communication, education, and problem solving as a family unit to implement.

Equity structure, which becomes a family issue when percentage share distribution does not favor equality, can be discussed by family members or dictated by the founder or CEO. Equal ownership by all members of the next generation may honor the family's commitment to equal treatment that nurtures all family members, but it does a terrible disservice to the need for simple, focused business leadership based on merit. Rules about owners being operators rather than absentee owners can also promote growth of the business and, not surprisingly, of family members. But when family rules are misapplied to the business, individuals are often stymied and made to pay a high price for their family membership privileges.

Many large, publicly held corporations that depend on family-owned businesses for distribution, retail, or service functions often insist on equity structures in their distributors that differentiate between siblings and between owner-managers and absentee owners. Majority ownership by one individual is encouraged because the record on the survival capacity of equally owned family enterprises is dismal.

Establish Boards to Review Performance

Much has been written by consultants and academics (Danco, 1975; Ward, 1987) about the absolute need for outside boards of directors in family-controlled businesses. Owners of businesses often engage in conversation about the advantages and disadvantages of such a body. Many owners, of course, know a friend of a friend who was ousted by his or her own board of directors after having created and grown the business.

What role can a board of directors, a board of advisers, or an asset board composed of family members have in regenerating the business and promoting its growth?

Outside Board of Directors. An outside board of directors is no guarantee of effective management of the firm. In family-owned businesses, even outside board members may get trapped by family dynamics. They are forced to take sides and thus contribute to the general paralysis of top management with regard to strategic redirection (as in the *Saturday Evening Post*–Curtis Publishing case discussed at the beginning of the book). Rubber stamping is a common pattern of dysfunctional boards. They do not perform a critical review of top-management decisions and their outcomes, which is a basic board responsibility.

Functioning properly, an outside board of directors can critique the absence of a coherent strategic response to the changing competitive situation. It can recommend the hiring of additional top management or the replacement of existing leadership. A board of directors can also press for a structural reorganization to save the company from sibling conflicts that cannot be resolved.

Entrepreneurial obsession and family cohesion often block small but necessary adaptations to a changing economic and social environment. What founder-entrepreneurs may experience as "booing from the bleachers"—or unfair criticism by active directors—may indeed be the first indication that the business is in trouble or that new opportunities lie ahead.

Outside boards of directors of entrepreneurial firms need to develop an appreciation for the uniqueness of entrepreneurial businesses, so that they may effectively consult on issues that entrepreneurs worry too much or too little about. Directors in family-owned businesses also need to have some understanding of the role of the family in the vision of growth. Only then can they value and respect some of the choices made by CEOs trying to promote the growth of the business and the health of the family simultaneously.

Board of Advisers. A board of advisers is not as controversial to owners and CEOs as an outside board of directors, because advisers lack legal responsibility for the conduct of company business. Nevertheless, they can make a significant contribution to the business's knowledge about markets, technology, competition, state-of-the-art management, economics, and so on.

The addition of a board of advisers to the structure of an $8 million midwestern family-owned business opened the company to contributions from professionals previously unavailable to this rural firm. The board also influenced decisions regarding acquisitions, compensation of employees, and relations with customers and forged a general management advisory team out of previously provincial, single-discipline experts.

Asset Board. An asset board represents and protects the individual and collective interests of owners. Such boards are relevant only to family-owned businesses in which the financial interests of ownership and the intentions of management may not overlap fully.

When it comes to stimulating business growth, asset boards often represent the case for liquidity and diversification of the estate. The timing of the formation of an asset board is therefore of particular importance. The board should be educated in the business—its finances and objectives—and should be functioning at optimum capacity way before it must deal with complex issues of succession, growth, or diversification. By promoting a balanced view of business and family interests (both where they overlap and where they do not), asset boards can promote balanced growth of the joint founder-business-family system. An acquisition by the business, for instance, can be contrasted with a dividend distribution to owners that allows individually tailored diversification through personal investments. Some rules of consensus, reflecting the need to "agree to agree" (Jonovic, 1982), need to be observed in the interest of family harmony and health.

It may be in the interest of continued growth of the business and the family in business that boards be split. Each next-generation member heading a business unit, division, or limited partnership may structure that business as a separate company with its own board of directors, board of advisers, and/or asset board. Alternatively, a single holding company or family-enterprise board can review the strategic direction and performance of several independent businesses. (See Figure 12.)

What works for one company at one point in time may not work for another. The growth requirements of the business and the conflict-resolution abilities of family members will determine which alternative is most appropriate to stimulating business growth and keeping the family healthy.

The Regeneration State

Regeneration is the most confusing, disruptive, and potentially painful period in the process of stimulating business growth at the crossroads. It is the stage at which creative destruction is appropriate. New systems may have to be developed to replace the

Figure 12. Boards Organized to Serve (A) Individual Companies and (B) a Holding Company or Family Capital Corporation.

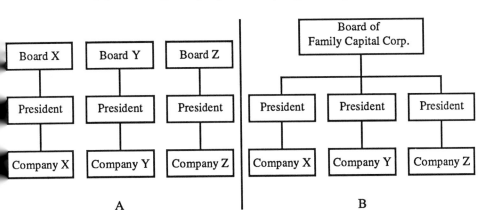

old. People's roles, responsibilities, and behaviors may have to change. Old habits may have to die. New coordination and planning mechanisms may have to be put in place. And as a result of all this changing, neither the old nor the new will work very well in the short term. Efficiencies may go down and profit margins may be squeezed.

The organization needs to mourn the death of the old ways. This requires time and saps motivation that could otherwise be aimed at promoting the desired growth. The questions everyone believed had been clearly answered months before are being asked again: Why do we want to grow? Is growth worth all this changing? Are we capable of managing the growth? Is this what the owners really want?

Resistance to creative destruction is present in different parts of the organization. Chances of its success are higher if the following conditions are met:

- There is a clear statement of the vision of growth.
- There is growing alignment with the vision and increasing commitment to this desired future state.
- A critical mass, a group of allies, is developing, and pockets of resistance are beginning to crumble.

- Action on the key people and systems identified by the PRISM is being taken.
- Rituals to mourn and let go of the old are allowed.
- Many people are involved in creating or making the new happen.
- An "orchestrated" set of change strategies is being used.

The regeneration state is a separate and distinct phase in the development of the organization. It is not the present state, but neither is it the envisioned growth phase. It is a distinct intermediate state that aims at restoring the organization to earlier dynamics of growth while allowing guidance by a new and unique vision.

Because it is a distinct state, it requires a unique governance and management structure. It also requires unique leadership: inspiring, courageous, and full of integrity.

Summary

Aligning the structure to allow a growth strategy to take hold and be implemented is essential. Structures can be either an obstacle to or a channeler of organizational energies. Organizational and financial structures that are aligned with the Growth Charter and that align family and business in the efficient pursuit of the chosen growth opportunity are critical—as critical to a regeneration at the crossroads as a clear vision and a sound growth strategy to which all are committed.

The objective of restructuring the organization during a period of regeneration is to increase the yield or value-added capability of the business under conditions of strategic change. In family-owned businesses, restructuring also serves to develop the managerial abilities of successors and helps reduce conflicts between potential successors and between founder and successor.

Businesses need vision, but they also need to have the capability to pursue this vision without undue hardship. Along with a strategy, organizational restructuring—in the total-system sense—is a key element in removing obstacles on the road to the vision of growth. Total system restructuring includes the following:

- Creating organizational structures appropriate to interpreneurship—for example, team structures, which promote growth.
- Aligning the family—its hierarchy/structure, culture, and behavior—with the requirements of the chosen business strategy.
- Realigning the capital structure of the firm by changing dividend policies, creating different equity types (preferred, voting, and nonvoting common stock), funding profit-sharing plans, employee ownership plans, and compensation plans, and by encouraging controlling ownership by owner-operators.
- Establishing active boards to review the strategy and performance of the firm and its management. Outside boards of directors, boards of advisers, and asset boards all review and positively influence different elements of the growth strategy.

The regeneration state is the period during which creative destruction takes place in the interest of promoting renewed growth. It is the most confusing, disruptive, and potentially painful period in the process of stimulating business growth. It is not the present state, but neither is it the envisioned growth state; rather, it is a distinct intermediate state that aims at restoring the organization to earlier dynamics of growth but guided by a new vision. Because it represents so much change, the regeneration state needs to be actively managed and requires a unique family and management governance structure.

Alignment of business and family with a commonly held vision and an actively understood and accepted strategy is essential to growth. I discuss how to develop this vision and the commitment to a growth strategy in Chapters Eight and Nine.

PART THREE

Ensuring Smart Growth and Continuity

Chapter Eight highlights the critical importance of a clear vision of growth to the process of making your business grow. A detailed picture of the future desired by the CEO, the owners, and other key managers is an essential ingredient of business regeneration. Mission statements provide identity and the foundation for creating a detailed growth plan.

A consensus- and commitment-building technique, the strategy-setting meeting, is the subject of Chapter Nine. Unlike traditional strategic plannng methods, the strategy-setting meeting shortens the period between gathering information for strategic analysis and implementing strategies. It has proven very effective in turning plans for growth into reality.

Chapter Ten surveys managerial practices that promote entrepreneurial activity across generations. Task or business teams, changes in compensation and information systems, diversification and specialization, particularly in areas where technology and market competency exist in-house, and entrepreneurial approximations can all be implemented to enhance successful business growth, as I explain here.

In Chapter Eleven, I suggest ten key strategies for CEOs and business owners committed to business growth. I go on to summarize key points from my own consulting experience and research into making businesses grow.

For readers interested in a quick survey of techniques available for financing new growth, Resource A at the end of the book sets forth several financial strategies that support business growth. A case illustrating the concepts of smart growth and interpreneurship can be found in Resource B, also at the end of the book.

8

Establishing a Clear Vision
for Growth

Growth, like other forms of change, produces a certain amount of pain, discomfort, and even confusion and disorientation. As a result, a new growth phase often takes place only after a significant crisis—for example, the death of the founder-entrepreneur, the absence of profits in the business, or a divorce in the family—has proven old ways inappropriate or untimely.

Growth can also result from a positive pull by the market-place or a vision of a very desirable future state. It is this impetus that most of us imagine when we think of growth; we picture a growth spurt triggered by exceptional market demand that astute owners and managers anticipated or somehow stimulated.

Dissatisfaction with the status quo and alignment with a desirable future state are both sources of energy for the growth of the business, as was discussed in Chapter Three. They are both important resources for a firm to cultivate in its efforts to overcome the tendency toward decline or paralysis in the face of a revitalizing course of action.

Once management has decided to grow the business, what obstacles will most likely be encountered? There is no greater barrier to growth than lack of consensus among owning family members about the desirability and the nature of growth sought. And there is no greater obstacle to this consensus than a founder-entrepreneur or second-generation CEO who does not have a life beyond the business. The CEO who is unable to "get passionate" about something other than the business simply cannot let go.

To the extent that the CEO links life and vitality exclusively to active involvement in the business, he or she blocks the next generation from responsible leadership in the business and fails to capitalize on the natural ebb and flow in product life cycles. (Product lines that ebb after a twenty- or twenty-five-year growth period present a unique opportunity for management changes that will lay the foundation for further growth of the business.) Paradoxically, precluding members of the next generation from taking an active leadership role in the business often leads that generation to pursue leisure activities with a passion—whether golf, alcohol, or vacation travel.

A CEO whose life revolves exclusively around the business will doom the business to his or her life span. And while founders can certainly pursue single-generation businesses if they choose, the implications for family members, employees, and communities are significantly different with short-lived endeavors than with intergenerational entities. Continued growth of both the business and the family is nearly impossible without the next generation's being allowed significant influence in the business while the previous generation is still alive and healthy.

The CEO (and founder) of a large independent insurance brokerage was recently wrestling with the choice of whether to let his son take over the business and stimulate its growth or whether to continue the role himself. Now sixty-nine, he has already tried once to retire to Florida and become passionate about tennis. But he could not. He is now quite emphatic about his inability to retire: "I just can't do it. I can't lose my power base; it's my life." (His own father, who had not been in the same business, had died right after retiring.) This founder quietly and not entirely deliberately undermined all efforts to regenerate the business. If he had been clearer to others and to himself about his choice, he would have spared family members and nonfamily managers and employees further pain and agony.

What Is a Vision?

In Chapter Three we considered vision as a part of the entire growth process. Because consensus around a vision is so crucial to the success of a growth strategy, however, let us now consider it in greater depth. For our purposes here, a vision is a clear, concise statement of what we want at some point in the future. The word *vision* is clearly tied to sight, so it is no surprise that the visual arts are often credited with providing a sense of the visionary in human experience. Throughout the ages, the visual arts have been the dominant medium for expressing humanity's most sublime visions, for making the spiritual, the important, and the transcendent visual through images. These visual metaphors give form and body to people's most cherished values and beliefs. The visual medium transforms an artist's personal creation into a public form in which others may participate. In the same way, a vision of business growth should be a visual metaphor that communicates a leader's creation and draws others actively into its aspirations for the future.

Visions combine strategic objectives and ways of doing business that constitute the essence or the "heart" of the organization. Visions highlight important results, not the processes or means of achieving them. Visions remain dynamic and living pictures that guide the day-to-day activities of masterful leaders. In *Zen and the Art of Motorcycle Maintenance*, Robert Pirsig (1974) describes the leading and dynamic quality of a worker's focused vision: "His motions and the machine's are in a kind of harmony. He isn't following any set of written instructions because the nature of the material at hand determines these thoughts and motions which simultaneously change the nature of the material at hand. The material and his thoughts are changing together in a progression of changes until his mind is at rest at the same time the material is right" (p. 128).

The "material" of business leaders is the organization. When their visions are realized, leaders rest and are renewed before the organization faces the next stage of growth and regeneration. The structural tension created by not having yet achieved the vision of a desired future state—the point where "the material is right"—is the source of growth energy that is absolutely critical to creating new corporate possibilities.

A new vision is often the product of a new generation of managers or the next-generation family members in family-owned businesses. New visions are potentially revolutionary, because they contain the seeds not just of a new branch but of an entirely new tree. But just as young trees are fortunate to be sheltered by healthy, established trees, young entrepreneurs are fortunate—and very smart—to grow in the shadow of the founding entrepreneur and his or her loyal customers and suppliers.

In family-owned businesses, many issues can prevent a new vision from taking root: sibling rivalry, an emotionally charged relationship between management and family, and the life stages of the CEO and next-generation aspirants to the job. Resistance from others may further polarize the next-generation entrepreneur and force him or her toward a radical stance; while the ghost of the founder, lingering around corners, in hallways, and in meeting rooms, erodes the confidence of the new generation in its own vision. Purposeful evolution, even if more appropriate to the business, may seem like a long shot to a new generation, unskilled in managing change and disrespectful of the historical wisdom that made the business what it is.

To nurture a new growth vision, both generations must be involved. The new generation must understand the history of the business, why current strategies were chosen, and what makes the business successful. It must want to build on this foundation to grow the business. The earlier generation, on the other hand, must strongly support—emotionally and financially—the new vision for growth. This support, necessary to preserve the health of the business and satisfy the need of the next generation to differentiate itself from the preceding one, must be unwavering in the face of mistakes, miscalculations, and even greater-than-expected success, with its accompanying stresses and strains on the business.

Why Is a Vision Necessary?

A commonly held vision creates alignment among different social groupings, business segments, staff and line functions, branches of the family involved in a family-owned business, different generations, and key individuals. Individuals and groups who have previously emphasized their differences, their angles, can now join together and jointly create growth to satisfy the mutually experienced structural tension, the pull, that a good vision provides.

Research has shown that firms reaching maturity and beginning the succession to a next generation face increasing complexity and potential for conflict (Dyer, 1986; Levinson, 1971). The CEO is generally not the awesome person the founder once was; a nonfamily professional manager in a second- or third-generation firm, for example, is decidedly human in the eyes of the owning family. The business has become a complicated network of outside investors, family members, and nonfamily employees—all with different aspirations.

These very different interests are accentuated by the power they assume under conditions of increased wealth. The value of the equity and the present value of dividends to family members now compete with the costs typically associated with financing growth. Conflict about whether to grow or not—and if so, at what rate and in what direction—is significant in most closely held companies and owning families facing the critical choice.

In this context, many experts argue, the major challenge facing mature companies is finding a way to bring people with diverse interests together to work for the good of the organization and the shareholders—that is, the challenge of developing a collective vision for growth. If regeneration is going to take place in the not-so-fertile phase of organizational maturity, high commitment to a Growth Charter is absolutely necessary.

Getting Started: Mission, Vision, and the Growth Charter

The CEO, other key managers, and family leaders must now begin to draw a mental picture—a vision—of what they want for themselves, their organization, and their family in anywhere from a three- to a ten-year timeframe. There is no need to be concerned about a long (say, greater than ten-year) timeframe, because people have a propensity to be too "lofty" on these; intermediate targets will make longer-term visions practical and actionable.

The focus of the vision work is *growth at the crossroads*. What follows is very much a workbook, a user's manual, for the development first of a mission statement and then of a vision and Growth Charter, which is the written statement of the vision of the future that a CEO and family in business want to create. The choice of words, the nuances, make a difference, just as they do in that well-known Growth Charter, the U.S. Constitution. The inalienable rights, as we know, are life, liberty, and the *pursuit* of happiness. Life and liberty are rights, but not happiness; only its pursuit is so designated. What a wise distinction! Imagine this country's founders dreaming about our collective national future separately, then together—arguing over words, trying to discover the full meaning of their aspirations for the future. This is the task that lies ahead for families in business. Let us get started.

Complementing Vision and Mission

A mission statement answers two questions: "What is our reason for being?" and "How do we want to do business?" In the mission statement, owners thus define, in writing, the nature of their commitment to the future of the enterprise. They also elaborate on family philosophy and articulate values that are important to family members in the conduct of business. The written mission statement has helped many entrepreneurial organizations retain high levels of motivation and commitment by owners and employees for years and has helped these companies exhibit continued innovation in both business and social processes. An excerpt from one such mission statement follows. (The business's name is omitted to preserve anonymity.)

Mission

To provide the best in quality and value in precision plastic injection molded products and services, recognizing and promoting the person as consumer, industrial customer and producer. And [to provide each associate] with opportunity for each to realize his or her highest potential.

This will result in: loyal customers, committed associates, the highest return on investment and business continuity through the generations.

How We Propose to Do This

Provide the best, by recognizing that our long-term success depends on providing our customers with the best in quality and value; in other words we must fulfill their specific desires and needs in a manner which is truly superior and commensurate with their investment in us. To continuously provide the best is not easy. It means constantly striving to improve on everything we do.

Recognize and promote the person as consumer, customer and producer. . . . Each of us depends on our associates for quality performance. And each of us has the responsibility to support our associates with nothing less than the best we have to offer.

The consumer is the ultimate user of the products we produce. . . . In fulfilling our mission, we are making possible the success of our customers. When our industrial customers receive quality and value from us, they are able to deliver quality and value to the final consumer. In a larger sense, we are all customers of each other. The next person in the production process is your customer, and the next one his. When each of us produces the best quality for our next customer, our mission is accomplished. . . . We believe, as producers, that work is a source of personal growth, satisfaction and enjoyment, as well as financial gain.

Since we trust and depend on each other, it is important that we communicate honestly and effectively. We believe that a free flow of information is essential to achieving our mission. Each of us can offer a unique perspective to the challenges we face. Each of us has the right and the responsibility to participate fully in solving problems and making decisions. . . .

A family mission statement preceded this family-business mission statement, and wisely so. Experience shows that, particularly in later-generation family businesses and those with several nonmanaging owners, the family mission statement is a good foundation for the family-business mission statement.

How to Arrive at a Mission Statement

The CEO needs first to slow down. Meditation or any other form of relaxed reflection may help. She needs to think about her purpose in life. What is her reason for being? The family's? The mental images that emerge will give the CEO clues about her calling, about those things that matter, and about what she does best. The CEO also needs to think about the contributions she wants to make in her lifetime and about those challenges she enjoys above all else.

Now what about the company's reason for being? Is it to

provide employment for family members, maximize profitability, ensure continuity, achieve higher returns on investment, serve the customer, or develop new markets for its existing products?

Whatever pictures emerge, in words or drawings, should be captured before they fade into a busy schedule. The resulting document will highlight management, family, and/or firm values that are central to the past, present, and future of the business—that is, the mission.

Visions of growth and regeneration complement the mission statement by developing a picture of where you want to be and what you want to accomplish within a particular timeframe. Visions guide growth plans and significant transformations in companies. Consider Kollmorgen Corporation (profiled more fully in Chapter Ten), a $350 million family business headquartered in Stamford, Connecticut, which believes that "freedom and respect for the individual are the best motivators of man, especially when innovation and growth are the objectives" (Kollmorgen Corp. Annual Report, 1979, p. 1). Its chairman of the board, Robert Swiggett, defines the vision of innovation as "technological leadership and first to market with the best" (p. 2). He also concretely defines growth as a "doubling of sales and earnings every four years while exceeding a 20% return on shareholders' average equity" (p. 3)—a significant feat, and one that Kollmorgen has actually accomplished.

A vision of the future that is rich in detail hooks the passion of any experienced or budding entrepreneur. Such a vision replaces the fear of risking or losing accumulated assets with the promise of a return. It replaces a problem orientation with enthusiasm about a whole spectrum of available opportunities, and a rear-view-mirror management mentality with anticipation over the next forward thrust of the business.

A leader who helps the organization and the owners or owning family articulate such a vision through his or her every action can pull the business into the future. After all, this kind of leadership is the key executive task of the CEO of a firm committed to growth. The firm must enroll all its members in the meaning and excitement of the future, and it must pull all of their individual energies into the creation of something larger than each individual is capable of creating alone.

How to Arrive at a Vision for the Company

Several steps are necessary for developing a vision for the company: personal vision, organizational vision, and a written Growth Charter.

Personal Vision. A vision answers the question, Where do I/we want to be, and what, that really matters, do I/we want to have accomplished in this particular timeframe? This step is essential for focusing energy for growth.

Now the CEO needs to see herself three (or five or ten) years from now. What is happening in the personal, family, business, and professional aspects of her life? It helps to be specific about details in terms of what, with whom, and so on, and to think in terms of results more than in terms of activities or processes. The vision should be written in the present tense—for example, "Today, March 27, 1994, I am . . ." Writing it in the present tense stimulates positive, creative tension that will help achieve the vision. Once "seen," this vision should be captured in words.

Organizational Vision. Now it is time to envision the family business three (or five or ten) years from now. What is happening? How does the company actually look? What has it just accomplished? Thinking in terms of results rather than activities or processes is again essential. Being specific about details in terms of what, where, and who is also important. Writing this corporate vision in the present tense again stimulates energy for growth: For example, "Today, March 27, 1994, Midwest Electronics is . . ."

Results in terms of profitability, return on investment, sales growth, new technology, customer relations, human resources, and relations with banks, suppliers, and the community are typically addressed in an organizational vision. The nature of the involvement of family members, quality of family relations, and individual accomplishments may also be covered.

The Growth Charter. The Growth Charter builds on the mission and vision developed and answers one further question: How does the family want to do business?

Here are excerpts from one such statement:

> There has been a trend toward increasing size of organizations. But we are convinced that the medium-size business has advantages that will make it survive. The needs that our firm responds to are unique. In serving these needs we discover our economic reason to exist.
>
> *Mission:* To grow steadily in our chosen markets by discovering and capably responding to the needs of our customers with a distinctly high-value product/service offering.
>
> *Customers:* To grow, we are providing superior quality products and customer service. Our competitors have been able to match our prices. But product quality and superior service from our knowledgeable and caring associates is giving us an edge. . . .
>
> *Associates:* We believe that people want challenging and meaningful work. When people know that they are making a difference, that they are contributing, they find meaning at work and derive satisfaction from their efforts. We are attracting and keeping the highest caliber people in the area because we respect our associates and consciously design work that motivates them. We promote an informal atmosphere and constant communications. Our size has remained under 200 people in every one of our locations precisely because that makes each one of our associates count. . . .
>
> *Growth:* We are doubling our sales and earnings every four years and are exceeding our initial goal of a 20 percent return on shareholders' equity. . . .
>
> *Family:* Only family members that truly wanted to work here and were at least as capable as other associates are involved in management today. This is a family company. We are all family here. And because we respect family life, we are minimizing moves and other disruptions to the deep commitment to families, communities, and balanced personal lives that we share. . . . [Growth Charter of a company whose name is withheld to maintain privacy.]

When a business develops a Growth Charter as a team of executives or as a family, it is useful to have each participant go through all four steps individually in preparation for an executive and/or family meeting. If much of the thinking and creating is done individually, meeting time is saved and the quality of the family's or management team's vision is improved. Group or committee work can be ineffective and wasteful of time without individual preparation and without a well-defined set of goals and tasks for participants to accomplish. These goals need to be identified and communicated by the group's leader, typically the CEO, in advance of the meeting.

If the CEO has started the process alone, communicating the vision to others is the next step. The CEO needs to say it, act it, be it, and repeat it. He needs to start engaging a few key others in this developing Growth Charter. He needs to recruit allies on his management team, in his family, and on the board. And once he experiences some successes in enrolling others, it is time to branch out to enroll still others.

It is important that CEOs developing a shared vision continue to listen to others' personal and organizational visions and learn from them. Differences of opinion made our Constitution a wiser document, after all. Besides, contributors make good allies. The CEO needs to start disseminating a draft of the Growth Charter widely throughout the family and the business to open dialogue. Management also needs to take small actions that support the Growth Charter *and learn from these.* If the actions are successful, the CEO needs to spread the word; if they are not, they can be used to improve the implementation of the charter. The CEO can then hold special meetings of employees or associates to focus on commitment to and implementation of the Growth Charter, as well as meetings of the owners to discuss their commitment to growth. Progress toward the Growth Charter can be communicated internally through one-pagers, videos, booklets, or special celebration events. Commitment to the Growth Charter should also be communicated externally—to customers, suppliers, and the community— perhaps by publishing a brochure on it.

Linking the Growth Charter to daily operational decision making in the business is key. The Growth Charter should also be linked to decisions made in the family. All family members and employees need to see the connection between the Growth Charter and their daily actions.

It is easy to lose sight of achievements in the pursuit of the vision, so progress reports should be scheduled regularly. And it is hard not to lose perspective about the vision in the process of reaching it. It is important that the business acknowledge the growth that the CEO, the CEO's allies, and the Growth Charter have stimulated.

Envisioning Growth in Quality and/or Quantity

Business folklore would have us believe that volume growth, like profits, is a paramount purpose of business owners and managers. My experience is quite the contrary. As consultant to family-owned and young entrepreneurial companies, I frequently advise a variety of founder-entrepreneurs and owners of small family businesses. Most of these business leaders appear quite committed to the beauty of smallness and simplicity. They want growth but do not purposefully run full throttle to stimulate it. To them, growth is a matter of degree, and it can be qualitative as well as quantitative in nature. So while some CEOs do not aspire to build billion-dollar cross-generational dynasties, they may aspire to greater national reputation or to a best-of-kind quality perception by customers. Recognizing the turbulence of competitive environments today, or realistically assessing the complexities of family life—especially family *business* life—these visionaries hold a less sizable growth objective than Kollmorgen's. Here are two examples:

Allen, Miller, and Partners, a professional services firm, was founded about thirty years ago by a graphic designer. The business provided the founder with a living during those thirty years; but more important for him, it provided a vehicle for making a difference in the visual arts community. Through the firm, he lent media support to worthy causes, supporting community nonprofit organizations and teaching the next generation of designers attending the City Institute of Art. In that role, the firm had a life for one generation: the founder's.

The business continued, but aspirations started to change as a second generation of family and extended (not blood-related) family members started to lay claim to the future of the organization. When the next generation, a twelve-person group of employee-owners, succeeded to management, they were interested in growth.

Growing in numbers much beyond their current size would have been highly undesirable, however. Instead, their vision encompassed qualitative growth—that is, increased national recognition and, of course, the higher fees that national recognition brings.

West Coast Hospital Supplies, a distributor, is also a second-generation business, although until five or six years ago it had a first-generation appearance. (First-generation family businesses often exhibit simple or functional structures, no divisional or product organizations, and little or no geographical expansion.) Because no second-generation family members were prepared for or interested in immediate succession, an outside manager was hired to preside over the business at least temporarily. The second-generation owner then went into semiretirement. The nonfamily general manager developed a growth vision that has, so far, been supported by the owner.

Prior to hiring the nonfamily member, the owner told me, "My wife and I make a nice living here. I like the community. My daughters are not interested in the business, and my son-in-law may or may not fit the bill. Who needs to push growth? Who needs all the stress? If I expand and start doing business in Arizona, I may get distracted in San Diego and make it easy for new competitors here." This owner, recognizing the value of growth to the business and the family but knowing that he lacked the will to engineer the growth himself, hired a nonfamily manager to lead the company through the growth process while the family sorted out interest and capability issues for succession.

Making a living for the family and making a contribution to the community are the aspirations of many founder-owners. Even when their visions point them toward greatness, they often describe proposed growth not in quantitative but in qualitative terms: quality of product, enhanced image and reputation, product and organizational innovation, increased competitive advantage, and increased colleagueship and family feeling in the organization.

These aspirations, like Kollmorgen's, are growth visions. But they are not expressed in typical terms of increased sales volume. In a comparative study of fifty large, well-established family companies and two hundred public companies, John Ward (1987) found that the family companies competed in smaller, more mature, and more regional markets on the basis of quality, specialization, customization, flexibility, and customer service by employees eager to serve. Growth in these firms does not therefore necessarily mean lowered costs and increased volume in a never-ending cycle. But it *does* mean continuous improvement and appropriate growth. The family firms Ward studied spent proportionately more than the public companies on research and development, marketing, and capital investment, even during economic downturns. This gave them more of a foothold on the future without detracting from their profitability. They achieved an average 26 percent return on investment, compared to a 21 percent return on investment for the public companies over the same sixty-year period (1924–1984).

Summary

A detailed picture of the future that is desired by the CEO and the family in business is an essential ingredient of a business regeneration. Visions need to be rooted in what people really want for themselves and for those related to them by kinship ties or work relationships in the family business. The development of vision requires discipline. Fragments of time spent thinking about the future will produce fragmentary and fleeting pictures of what is most important.

The visions of everyone in management and ownership need to be communicated—shared and discussed—and a consensus needs to be reached. A big block to such a consensus is a CEO's refusal to "hang his hat" and give the next generation real opportunities to influence the future of the family business before its late thirties. Both generations are essential to a good vision, because both the wisdom of tradition and the wisdom that knows when to break with tradition need to be fused into *one vision of the future*.

A family mission statement and a family-business mission statement are the first steps in the development of a common vision of the future. These provide identity and a platform for important family values. Visions of growth complement these with targets for the accomplishment of significant results in the chosen growth path.

A Shift of Mind and Heart: The Will and the Passion to Grow

The vision of growth may include objectives of growth in the size of the business and its operations, or more qualitative growth objectives, such as improved quality of product, increased reputation, or the best customer service in the industry.

Growth has to be in the heart and the mind. When management lacks the will to grow, businesses often stagnate. If and when a next generation joins the business, the task of stimulating business growth is much more complex. But a new generation may create a serendipitous overlap between the business's need to grow and the needs of family members to venture out into their own territories. Actually, that overlap is rarely caused by serendipity: rather, it is due to family and firm finding a way jointly to optimize the growth imperatives of the family, management, and ownership systems.

9

Using Strategy-Setting Meetings to Turn Plans into Smart Growth

The past several years have seen development of the strategy-setting meeting, an activity that allows an owner and management group to review the results of its competitive and strategic planning analysis in order to "own" and commit to appropriate action. Because its emphasis is on action, the technique helps move the firm from the planning to the implementation of growth opportunities. A consultant, acting as facilitator, is recommended.

The strategy-setting meeting is conceptually rooted in Richard Beckhard's (1987) work on transition management and large-system change and constitutes a new application of his widely used "confrontation meeting" technique (1967).

The Meeting's Agenda

Strategy meetings among owners and top managers have traditionally generated energy and focus. The resulting esprit de corps is too often dissipated as the planning process attempts to include nonmanaging owners and lower-level employees in the organization. A significant amount of additional time is then invested in strategy communication meetings and similar efforts to bring others on board.

The strategy-setting meeting can be carried out in six and a half or seven hours of working time with anywhere from thirty to one hundred people across the entire organization (although a particular business may choose to limit attendance to the owning family, or to owners and top management only).

Below is an annotated agenda for the day-long meeting. Not all of the information mentioned will be available to every firm, and recommended times are approximate only.

1. Introduction and Climate-Establishment (first thirty to forty-five minutes). The owner or top manager communicates to the total group his or her goals for the meeting, establishes the groundrules, and assures the group that there will be no negative consequences for expressing disagreement or alternative perspectives.

A brief presentation by the owner, the top manager, the manager of planning, or the consultant can help to set a conceptual base for the day's activities. A review of recent studies, a planning framework, or a business policy case may be used too. It is also helpful if the manager of planning or the consultant describes the process that will take place.

2. Sharing of Planning Information (thirty to forty-five minutes). The executive responsible for the planning and development function in the company presents a summary of the strategic information available to the firm, including information on economic forecasts, price trends for key raw materials, trends of suppliers, government regulations, activities of relevant consumer groups, the changing nature of the industry, competitors' costs, and market shares. The executive also discusses the relative strengths and weaknesses of the firm and its competition. What emerges is a profile of the competitive challenges currently faced and expected in the future. The use of graphs, colorful displays, and vignettes that all present can relate to increases the impact of the planning "homework" on the strategy-setting activities that follow. (For an excellent guide to the analytical "homework," see Ward, 1987).

3. Strategy Information Analysis (sixty to ninety minutes). The large group is now divided into small, heterogeneous groups of

seven or eight people. Owners and top management separate from
the rest of the group and meet either separately or together. Each
small group should represent a "diagonal slice" of the organization:
members of these smaller groups should come from different
departments or functional units, as well as from different levels of
management. No boss/subordinate pairs should be in the same
group.

The task here is to involve every participant in determining
the maturity of the industry of which the company is a part, the
basis of competition in this industry, and the range of strategies that
may be available to the firm. The outcome of these discussions is a
definition first of where the business is now, then where the group
wants to take it, in terms of both qualitative and quantitative
(financial) shifts in the nature of the business.

After the discussion, the group writes a summary strategy
statement that reflects the thematic outcomes of its discussion.
Typically, group participants find enough common threads in their
thinking to serve as the basis for a paragraph that can be agreed
upon. The group needs to check its summary for internal consistency between financial measures (such as return on investment,
cash flow, market share, and earnings growth) and positioning
factors (such as relative quality or relative price).

4. Strategy Statement Presentations (sixty minutes). Each
small group, as well as the owner/management group(s), presents
its strategy statement. A consensus statement is then arrived at under
the leadership of the planning manager, key owner(s), or consultant. This statement clearly has to meet with the approval of the
owners and other top management.

Broad statements, while not providing the degree of direction
often expected by participants, are not to be automatically
discouraged. The themes here presented may contain the seeds for
much change, affecting relationships and power in the business and
the family and thus threatening the CEO's need for an orderly
transformation of the company. This first draft can therefore afford
to be somewhat vague.

5. Functional Groups' Mission and Strategic Action Plan
(ninety minutes). The total group is now divided into departmental

groups (for example, personnel, finance, engineering) to answer these three questions:

1. What is our unit's mission in obtaining strategic advantage for the firm? How can we help the company get there?
2. Based on the company's strengths/weaknesses and the threats and opportunities posed by the competitive environment, to what specific strategic action can we commit ourselves?
3. To what issues, problems, and obstacles should the top-management team give highest priority?

These unit meetings are led by the functional unit manager. He or she should encourage new ideas and alternatives but be on the lookout for commitments that appear impractical or unrealistic in a given timeframe.

Participants should stop short of preparing detailed operating plans or weighing budget considerations; these are follow-up activities for which a staff person may assume data-gathering responsibility.

6. Strategic Action Plan Presentations (one to two hours). The departments then present their commitment plan and point out obstacles that could be overcome with the help of other functional units or of top management. Owners and top management provide a reality check by asking what-if questions. They may also form cross-functional task forces to further investigate resource allocation issues or follow up on implementation. Someone— perhaps the planning manager or the consultant—should then summarize the day by listing the ten or twelve critical operating actions to be taken this year in support of the strategy.

7. Communicating the Results of the Meeting (forty-five minutes). Participants now decide how to communicate the results of this meeting to any subordinates who were absent. Communication plans are drawn up by each functional subgroup. These plans are shared briefly with the total group.

8. Closing. The owner, top manager, or consultant then wraps up the meeting after a date has been set for a follow-up.

Management may then choose to adjourn for a smaller meeting behind closed doors. Some delicate issues may require this kind of treatment as part of the strategy-setting meeting.

At a progress review held six to eight weeks later—generally a two- or three-hour follow-up meeting—the full group reviews commitments, and further managerial or ownership action is taken as appropriate. Links to the operating budget are reviewed for consistency between strategy and resource allocation.

Strategy-Setting Case Studies

I first created the strategy-setting meeting to meet the needs identified by the president of the consumer products division of a corporation. Because the division had recently been formed, he felt that it had to develop its own identity, business strategy, and commitment of its people to its new strategy.

The division had traditionally contributed handsomely to the earnings of the larger corporation. But new growth opportunities were now envisioned, so more aggressive competitive behavior in the marketplace appeared to be in order. Initial support for this premise had created the new division, but the president was concerned that, unless the new strategy was widely developed and committed to, neither his subordinates nor the company owners would fully understand and back the new business charter to the extent that it needed to be supported.

He saw the strategy-setting meeting as an opportunity to involve, in a short period of time, the owners and large numbers of managers and employees in the newly formed company, as well as key staff from the corporation's main office.

The technique proved effective in engaging people in the possibilities of a very exciting future for the company. It also generated so much enthusiasm that some of the participants emerged from the meeting worried about having overcommitted themselves or their departments.

To address this concern, top management was encouraged to respond with more than passive agreement to the progress review presentations scheduled six weeks later. Management was asked to critically question the availability of resources and the feasibility of the time horizons agreed to.

In retrospect, this progress review seems to have contributed more than just a reality check. By agreeing to a follow-up meeting during the course of the first activity, management gave a strong signal that the strategy-making process initiated by this day-long meeting was not a one-time event.

Approximately eight months later, a second opportunity to use the strategy-setting meeting approach—this time with a midsized family-owned company in Latin America, a large exporter of cocoa powder and cocoa butter—presented itself to me. The president of the company (and son-in-law of the founder) was concerned that very profitable opportunities in world markets had led the sales department to commit the company to delivery volumes and deadlines that were totally unrealistic for the manufacturing plant. Months of pressure and extensive overtime work were causing fatigue and promoting an attitude that quality did not matter.

The president saw a real need to reestablish a strategic imperative of the business: to consistently manufacture a high-quality product. Consistent quality allowed the producers to charge more for their product and thus extract a higher profit from a limited crop. He also saw the need for the top-management team, which included a couple of other family members, to commit itself to the strategy of the business without pursuing attempts to gain favor in the eyes of the founder.

Using a strategy-setting meeting, the top-management team and middle management openly discussed and worked through the problems the sales department was creating for manufacturing and manufacturing was creating for sales. They talked about the impact this cross-departmental pressure was having on the quality and image of the product and on the lives of the overworked production employees (who had been unable to spend a weekend with their families for months in a row). The meeting team issued a new competitive position statement and developed a new manufacturing strategy that day.

Strategic Management Advantages

Perhaps the clearest benefit of the strategy-setting meeting is that objectives and strategies that are unknown, confused, and/or forgotten can be clarified. Because the meeting process is managed, the strategy-setting meeting replaces haphazard, trial-and-error meeting formats that often lead to endless and fruitless strategic discussions. Opening the process to greater involvement also enhances the quality of strategies by guarding against the "group-think" of the top-management team.

Systematic improvements in the strategic management process include successful handling by management of an increased number of internal organizational obstacles to the new strategy, increased consensus among owners about the attractiveness of particular growth opportunities, the reporting of competitive information to more people throughout the company, and the renewed reliance on internal ventures, market experimentation, and customer-oriented market research to find the answers to competitive questions.

Some firms have also seen benefits to initiating parallel planning organizations—a network of task forces and business teams—to maintain the focus on strategy and its implementation.

Other companies have created these groups for a shorter-term, tactical purpose. For example, a large bank holding company, in which branch improvement teams surveyed customer satisfaction, disbanded these as soon as their project was completed.

Companies without a strategic planner on board (as is often the case in family-owned businesses) have often chosen a strategy czar at the strategy-making meeting. This person, often a successor, then becomes the focus for continuing strategy-making activity in the firm.

The strategy-setting meeting is showing promise in the critical task of increasing commitment to strategy implementation and reducing the terrible waste and dissipation of an organization's management energy and a family's nurturing energy.

Businesswide Advantages

In addition to strategic management improvements, the strategy-setting meeting also has some organizationwide advantages:

1. A real dialogue is initiated between owners, top management, and middle management, which personalizes both top management and the firm's strategy. This is a particularly important advantage in family-owned firms, where it is critical to develop a culture that maintains organizational cohesiveness regardless of family dynamics.
2. Collaborative strategy setting between several levels and functions is demonstrated and practiced. Participants report understanding strategic planning and strategies better than ever before.
3. Larger numbers of people feel "ownership" of the future of the firm, because of their involvement in and contribution to the setting of the strategy.
4. The top-management team can take immediate corrective action based on the sound intelligence of concerned employees who track competitors' moves. A credibility of intentions is established between various levels of management when owners and top managers make real commitments in the strategy-setting meeting and establish progress review checkpoints.
5. By requiring that different levels and departments trust their interdependence, the strategy-setting meeting clearly has a positive impact on the overall organizational culture.
6. The strategy-setting meeting is generally a success experience. To the extent that the momentum is maintained through periodic progress reviews, confidence and morale improve. A can-do attitude replaces a planning paralysis in many firms' staff, operating management, and family asset boards.

When to Use the Strategy-Setting Meeting

The strategy-setting meeting has been particularly helpful in situations where there are large numbers of owners and managers who are critical to the effective implementation of strategy. It also succeeds when it is difficult to take time from this busy group for any considerable stretch.

The strategy-setting meeting agenda presented earlier has been used in organizations of various sizes facing different competitive situations. Experience shows that it is most appropriate where the following conditions prevail.

1. There is a recognized need for the owner or owner-manager to review and commit to the implementation of the strategic plan.
2. Very limited time is available for the activity, and cascading strategy communication meetings have proven time-consuming but not very effective.
3. There is a recognition that although more planning will not improve the company's ability to succeed in its chosen strategy, widespread commitment to that strategy will.
4. The strategic analysis work has been done. The strategy-setting meeting is not a substitute for thorough study and analysis of competitive data, visionary leadership, and a lot of listening to customers, dealers, suppliers, distributors, and family members.
5. The organization is experiencing or has recently experienced the need for a new strategy or a significant strategic redirection.

A potential problem in the use of the strategy-setting meeting is that it is indeed a technique. As such, it may be used without the benefit of the art of management. To deprive this approach of the experimentation and the ongoing accountability associated with other managerial responsibilities is certain to make it less effective. Accountability is a prerequisite for line-management ownership of the strategic management process.

Summary

Strategic changes, popular wisdom says, have to be accompanied by changes in organizational structure and culture if they are to be successful. After major organizational changes, firms tend to experience considerable confusion, loss of energy, and loss of a sense of urgency. This phenomenon undermines the organization's productivity and its ability to stay focused on and committed to the new strategy.

At the crossroads, the CEO needs quick and efficient ways of reaching out and getting the rest of the organization and the owners to focus their energy on the most important strategies of the business. Failure to do so seems to subject firms to a period of reduced market share, lower profitability, and poor employee morale.

The traditional strategic planning approaches lengthen the period between getting the strategic analysis information and implementing the strategies. They also fail to involve many people who are key to managing strategically: owners and key lower-level managers, for instance.

The day-long strategy-setting meeting can provide the entire owning and/or management group with the following:

1. Important information about the objectives and strategies of the firm—information that clarifies direction and answers questions about the future.
2. A meeting agenda that, when properly used, is far preferable to haphazard trial-and-error meeting formats and endless discussions.
3. The opportunity for departments and divisions or business units to clarify their role in achieving and sustaining strategic advantage in the marketplace, and to set priorities accordingly.
4. Quality strategies improved by the many and varied sources of knowledge and expertise present in the meeting.
5. Greater commitment to the implementation of growth strategies by owners who have not been active in management and key employees throughout the entire organization.

Creating a new synthesis out of the business entity and the owning group is a many-faceted effort. Our discussion has taken us through a parallel course that joins together business and family in agreement on a strategy for the business and its continued growth. A sound strategy that is rooted in an owner's vision and long-term commitment to the future of the business is hard to beat. The next two chapters rest on this foundation.

10

Managerial Practices
That Support Innovation
and Growth

Before discussing managerial practices that weave interpreneurship into the fabric of an organization, let us review, with an eye toward implementation, the barriers to interpreneurship.

Barriers to Interpreneurship

Most obstacles to interpreneurship could be labeled bureaucratic in nature. Bureaucracy, or the natural hardening of organizational arteries that comes with age, plays a part in slowing down growth. Unhealthy family dynamics and inappropriate managerial practices and organizational structures also put on the brakes. Presented below and in Table 5 are several barriers to interpreneurship.

Absence of a Growth Vision. Most entrepreneurs feel impelled by a force that they themselves do not understand. Some call it heart; others call it passion or a crazy obsession. Because obsessions are not hereditary, if neither the preceding nor the following generation in an organization has a vision of long-term growth, the possibility of interpreneurship is very slim.

Table 5. Barriers and How to Overcome Them.

Identifying and Managing Barriers to Growth	Specific Interventions	Outcomes
Absence of growth vision	Specialization or diversification Entrepreneurial approximations	
Distance from customers, employees, operations, and the competition	Task and business teams	
"Nervous money" and short-term focus	Reward systems Family venture-capital company	Profitability Growth Family Harmony
Large overhead Obsession with data and rational logic	Information systems	
Perception of high social (image) risk Inappropriate boundaries between management, owners, and the interpreneur	Ownership equity structures Human resource policies and practices	

Distance from Customers, Employees, Operations, and the Competition. Family businesses such as Mars, Inc., Bechtel, Inc., and Kollmorgen stay close to their customers by engaging with them on new product ideas, product enhancements, and related opportunities. Eric von Hippel (1978) first documented the extensive use of this practice by a few companies, calling it the "customer-active paradigm." Similarly, companies committed to interpreneurship avoid anything that distances people within the organization, be it reserved parking spaces, titles, walls, lack of information, or "silver spoons." Families committed to interpreneurship are obsessive about communication and promote the personal growth and professional development of family members and nonfamily managers and employees.

"Nervous Money" and Short-Term Focus. Patience and timing are important skills whenever money is invested. New strategic directions are quite fragile until they take root and develop their own momentum and a critical mass of support. It takes time and it takes money to regenerate the vitality of any business. Creating a venture-capital arm and reorganizing the company into separate growing and mature divisions can help overcome this obstacle.

Large Overheads. The previous generation of owners or managers should not allow the interpreneur to "avoid the pain" of creating something new. Limiting funding of any new venture helps instigate creative "scrounging" or "bootlegging" by the entrepreneur, replicates external market conditions, and sharpens the focus of the interpreneur's creative process. However, this same constricted funding situation means that the interpreneur's project area should be shielded from the burden of taking on the mature corporation's overhead expenses. Just as the entrepreneur usually starts in a low-overhead, inexpensive, and inelegant office space, the interpreneur should be allowed the freedom to start with a minimum of previous financial commitments. For similar reasons, the interpreneurial area should be minimally staffed, especially reducing the number of support personnel; in this way, it imitates the startup situation of a firm composed of peer professionals.

Perception of High Social (Image) Risk. While not a family business, Exxon provides a good example of external-perception barriers to entrepreneurial activity within established businesses. When Exxon renamed Jersey Enterprises Exxon Enterprises, entrepreneurial employees felt the social pressure to perform in acceptable-to-Exxon ways. In his study of entrepreneurial management, Howard Stevenson (1985) of the Harvard Business School found the increased weight of what he called "social contracts" bearing down on managers in ways that prevented full consideration of opportunities. Instead of adventurousness, trusteeship of resources and constituencies became preeminent. Families in business are often highly visible in their own communities and need to create boundaries that allow them to free up time and resources to experiment without high social risk. Locating new businesses in different cities and giving them different names can help in this respect.

Obsession with Data and Rational Logic. Computers have made a bias toward data and rational logic much easier to pursue. The quantity and sophistication of financial software and the misuse of fashionable statistical process-control methods of business management prevent movement along the disorderly incremental path to new interpreneurial territory. The care and feeding of interpreneurs with a passion is more important than the standardized application of methods throughout the entire business. Interpreneurs need the freedom to follow their hunches. It might be appropriate to cordon off an area for them that is not as controlled as the rest of the business (control being vital to the more established segments of the business).

Inappropriate Boundaries Between Management, Owners, and the Interpreneur. It is difficult for people wearing different hats in different settings to be perceived appropriately in each setting. Is John, the successor, treated as John the son or John the aggressive interpreneur? And how can preconceptions and their accompanying role expectations be managed? When the boundaries between family and business are unclear, the family relationships may seem to be threatened by interpreneurial changes in the business.

Joseph Schumpeter (1962), an early writer on entrepreneurship, described entrepreneurship as the process of "creative destruction." The difficult destruction that is needed within a business to create something better is even harder to do when the business system is entwined with a family system. A brother who is the chief executive of the family business may have to balance the task of interpreneuring with managing the shifts that occur in his relationship with a younger brother working in the business as the business is reorganized. Executing the responsibilities of an interpreneur while having to meet relationship expectations or fulfill psychological contracts that are based on the son role often creates serious dilemmas. Such dilemmas can paralyze individuals and bring interpreneurial activity to a halt.

Interventions Aimed at Increasing Interpreneurship and Promoting Growth

After recognizing existing barriers and considering necessary changes in strategy, organization, finances, and the family, owners have to intervene directly in these areas. Interpreneurship requires overcoming the barriers listed earlier and shaping the systems and structures that will institutionalize the process of renewing or revitalizing the business. (See Tables 5 and 6.)

Diversification or Specialization. Unless the original market niche is growing, smart growth often requires diversification or further specialization. A must for successful diversification is knowledge of the market, the product, and the manufacturing process technology involved. As we stressed in Chapter Five, a policy of every growth-seeking entrepreneurial organization should be to "stick to its knitting"—that is, commit only to ventures where the company already has accumulated knowledge about customers, technologies, or ideally both.

There have been many studies exploring diversification, its outcomes, and the conditions under which it is most likely to be successful. Unrelated diversification, or diversifying into businesses or industries not related to the initial core business, is generally riskier. Research on diversification (Rumelt, 1982; Roberts and Berry, 1985) clearly shows that diversification that "sticks to one's knitting" pays off. Most diversification outside of the boundaries of products, manufacturing processes, and markets that are well known by the firm fails.

But the risks of unrelated diversification have been exaggerated because, in search of growth, owners and managers have often behaved like bankers or venture capitalists rather than obsessed entrepreneurs. Putting sweat equity into something you care enough about to support financially (on a shoestring) is very different from investing in a diversified portfolio of stocks.

Several rules based on this research should help diversification efforts. First, companies should not diversify unless they have to, to grow or preserve the profitability of the business or to offer interpreneurial opportunities to a promising next generation.

Table 6. Creating an Interpreneurial Culture.

	Requirements	Interventions
Growth Opportunity	1. Knowledge of product and manufacturing process technology	1. Specialization
	2. Knowledge of market	2. Diversification
	3. Overcoming the absence of growth vision	3. Entrepreneurial approximations
Organization	1. Role differentiation and separation between family and business and between owners and managers	1. Task and business teams
	2. Focused structures	2. Reward systems
	3. Communication and problem solving	
	4. Overcoming the distance between customers and employees	
Finances	1. Creation of an information-rich decision-making environment	1. Information systems
	2. Funding of new ventures	2. Family venture-capital company
	3. Overcoming the obsession with data and the "nervous money" syndrome	
Family	1. Equity structures that support "focused" organization structure and a distinction between active and inactive owners	1. Ownership equity structures
	2. Commitment and a sense of ownership by nonfamily employees	2. Human resource policies and practices
	3. Overcoming the inappropriate roles and boundaries between founder, family, and business	
	4. Overcoming the perception of high social risk	

Second, a business should not think of acquisitions, mergers, or new ventures unless the profit margins in those businesses are at least as good as those of the core business. It is easy to fall for the "grass is greener on the other side" phenomenon.

Third, the firm that plans to diversify via equity positions, mergers, or acquisitions needs to distinguish between investing and committing to growth through new ventures. A company that spent several million dollars in twelve companies through the early 1980s had returns of over $200 million in cash and stock but not a single major profitable new business unit.

Fourth, no one should diversify quickly into an area of business where the market or the technology is alien to the firm. The batting average is good only when management knows both, and gradually deteriorates as the firm steers farther and farther away from the company's area of expertise. Consider an insurance company that lost a lot of money when it diversified into construction. The son of the company's founder developed a new interest in construction as a result of managing a construction project for the company. Father and son colluded on this ill-fated diversification move for different reasons: the founder wanted to give the son a territory where he could pursue his own interests without interfering with the founder's domain; and the son was driven by the need to differentiate himself from his father—the need to be his own man. In the absence of product, manufacturing process, and market knowledge, better interpreneurial growth opportunities are venture-capital investments, joint ventures, or licenses.

Fifth, the business should set up a competent venture review board. Many of the benefits of diversification observed in conglomerates may be due to the supervision provided by top management that has strategic oversight responsibility to a unit of a larger corporation (Lauenstein, 1985). While units of conglomerates must justify their decisions to higher-ups, family businesses often lack such supervision.

Sixth, specialization is also a very viable growth opportunity, especially if most of a firm's profits come from only one or two of its product lines. While this growth opportunity seldom leads to sales volume growth, it often results in increased profitability and focus, a great foundation for renewed growth. Specialization typically cashes in on customers' needs for higher quality and customer service in exchange for higher prices. This is well-known strategic territory for many family businesses.

A final word of caution. Venturing into new businesses is obviously not an easy task; the casualty rate is high. But the guidelines summarized below should result in more encouraging statistics of success.

1.　Don't diversify unless you have to.
2.　Don't acquire, merge, or venture except for better profit margins.
3.　Distinguish between passive investments and active business ventures.
4.　Stay with familiar markets and technologies.
5.　Set up a competent venture review board.
6.　Consider a specialization in a high-quality, high-service niche.
7.　Remember that new ventures are risky!

Entrepreneurial Approximation. An excellent example of the creation of an entrepreneurial approximation is that of Mars, Inc. As was noted in Chapter Four, the founder, Frank Mars, made arrangements for his son, Forrest Mars, to start a new business in England. Forrest traveled abroad with several thousand dollars of family venture capital and the recipe for Milky Way, which became the Mars Bar in England. The European company grew at a very fast pace and in 1964 bought out its American counterpart.

One recent study (Biggadike, 1979) found that it takes an average of eight years for a corporate venture to reach profitability, and about ten to twelve years for its return on investment to equal that of mainstream business activities. However, when independent entrepreneurs start businesses, they reach profitability in four years—half the time (Weiss, 1981). The contrast between these two studies points to two things: the need for medium- to long-term financial support of any new venture sponsored by a business or family, and the need for better entrepreneurial structures within established companies (Drucker, 1985a).

Forming joint ventures with other entrepreneurial businesses, where (for example) financial support of the other firm's more promising research and development is exchanged for stock or licensing agreements, is another interpreneurial opportunity.

Task and Business Teams. Another organizational innovation that supports continued growth is that of task and business teams. Organized around a particular task or business unit—for example, new-product development, or business for a particular major customer—these teams are composed of representatives of various departments and top management as needed. Planning, doing, and reviewing are all responsibilities of these teams. Usually embedded in the context of a functional organization, they help a firm become more responsive to change, more adaptable to rapid growth, and more efficient in the deployment of human resources.

A Utah firm started such cross-functional teams along customer lines. Their concern was that rapid growth would lead to deterioration in product quality, on-time delivery, and manufacturing cost control. With a production manager acting as team leader and a team composed of representatives from engineering, finance, quality assurance, personnel, purchasing, and distribution, the firm has significantly improved on-time delivery and shortened order-to-delivery cycles. These changes have saved on the amount of cash-flow tied up in work-in-process inventory. The plants now operate with a strong customer focus. Top management periodically meets with this team to review accomplishments and do what it can to support continued improvement.

Still experimenting with interpreneurship and undergoing the test of time is Kollmorgen Corporation (introduced in Chapter Eight). Robert Swiggett, its chairman of the board, believes that in order to achieve innovation and growth, a company must maintain a "free market environment for every individual in the company" (Kollmorgen Corp. Annual Report, p. 1). That way, he argues, "each employee is exposed to the risks and rewards of the market" (p. 3). He or she succeeds or fails on the basis of skills and abilities in meeting this responsibility. And Kollmorgen believes that the best way to encourage such entrepreneurial commitment is to break a company into small, autonomous product or profit-center teams.

Kollmorgen found its vision of the future operating within its own confines—in the proto (for prototype) department, a small unit (thirty-five people) that could turn around an order for a new type of circuit board in one to three weeks. It generally took six to ten weeks for other departments to do the same. The speedy proto department was also the most profitable unit of the company. Ironically, though, it took several years for top management to realize that this small, renegade department had all of the components of what is now the Kollmorgen philosophy: small groups of committed individuals, acting autonomously (and often innovatively) to serve the customer, result in profitability and growth.

Kollmorgen's compounded rate of growth between 1974 and 1984 was a staggering 18 percent. Since then, in perhaps the worst electronics industry recession in twenty years, the company's profit margins have narrowed and its growth has slowed. But Kollmorgen intends to continue to grow, even if at a slower rate, and to produce a 20 percent return on equity for its shareholders. While other families in business could develop and promote a vision like that at Kollmorgen, family interests and desires need to complement the aspirations set for the business. As a result of these other interests, rates of growth may or may not be as aggressive. Marriott, another family-controlled business, has also been able to maintain annual revenue growth rates of about 20 percent.

Reward Systems. To support the growth strategy Kollmorgen managers had set for themselves, a new bonus plan was set up. This plan was driven by return on net assets, or RONA. RONA also gave individuals throughout the company a handy way of keeping score. Individuals in a division having a reasonably good year would end up with an additional 15 to 20 percent of their gross annual salaries paid to them in the form of a bonus. Within six months of the plan's implementation, receivables and inventories had been reduced by $11 million. On the long road to growth and continued entrepreneurship, significant short-term improvements were also evident. Kollmorgen's success illustrates that long-term business growth and short-term effectiveness can go together.

Pay is a strong incentive for risk taking and growth. This is particularly true in family businesses, where career opportunities for nonfamily employees may be limited.

Information Systems. Keeping up-to-date measures of company performance, coupled with dividing the larger enterprise into small business units, ensures that timely information about inventories, costs, customer wants, and competitor moves reaches every employee. This contact with the market environment is an information-rich decision-making context, where strategies and decisions are constantly updated and tested on the basis of new information.

Knowledge of the competition is particularly important in guiding growth and interpreneurship, because competitive information may contain the seeds of opportunities available to the business. At the Detroit bottle manufacturer and distributor mentioned earlier, the thirty-year-old fourth-generation president of the plastic bottles division frequently comes into the office with samples or cardboard displays of new product ideas. Combing through product shows and hardware and discount stores daily, he begins his days back at the office by laying out competitive product information for all to see. He tells everybody what is going on in the marketplace, what customers are thinking, and what new products he is considering. This practice is of particular value to family-owned businesses. Because of the close attachments of family life, a family business may focus predominantly on internal indicators and may ignore, deny, or minimize external information, with serious implications for market competitiveness.

Family Venture Capital Company. Infrequently tried, and yet quite promising for interpreneurship and continued growth, are the formation of venture-capital firms (such as the Rockefellers' Venrock), the formation of new-ventures divisions within businesses (often headed by successors), and the creation of ownership and reward systems that encourage long-term growth of the firm.

American Research and Engineering, a family business in Chicago, has set up a trust to enable the next generation to engage in entrepreneurial activity. Recognizing that the family business is often shaped by the personality of its founder and may therefore prove a poor fit for the succeeding generation, American's founder created a venture trust. Guided by the family philosophy ("You get out of life what you put in"), the trust enables any child in the family to be funded on a business venture of his or her own choosing. The individual must present a business plan for review by a board of family members, who decide whether to fund the endeavor or not. If the plan is accepted, the entrepreneurial family member receives the startup funds in exchange for 49 percent of the shares of the company.

With 51 percent of the shares, the interpreneur owns the company and returns to the family trust a dollar for every dollar of profit retained by the company. This helps fund children, cousins, nieces, or nephews down the road (Liataud, 1983). Tax law changes make the counsel of expert advisers acquainted with the particular situation a requirement in implementing funds of this sort.

The family's ability to assess the quality of investments and willingness to invest in them long term are critical to sponsor new ventures. Some families will never be able to act as venture-capital firms for the next generation. But many more could than currently do, if they would commit to a vision of growth and interpreneurship during the high-profitability years of the family business.

Ownership Equity Structures. The family capital corporation model mentioned earlier is a particularly attractive ownership structure, because of its ability to accommodate the needs and preferences of different individual owners. This financial structure can contain all of the assets of the family—both active business interests and passive assets (such as real estate and stocks in public companies). If the firm issues several classes of preferred and common stock, different owners can achieve their objectives without disrupting the continuity of the active business. Class A preferred stock, for instance, could be nonvoting and low par value, with a high dividend preference and liquidation preference after Class B preferred. As such, it would be perfect for a nonmanaging owner. Class B preferred could then have liquidation preference over all stock classes, have dividend preference after Class A, have voting rights that lapse at death, and be convertible to common stock. The common stock could have voting rights and receive all capital appreciation and possible future control.

A number of entrepreneurial privately held and family-owned businesses have chosen to distribute some equity to employees out of the conviction that the best way to get people to behave as owners do is for them to *be* owners. After all, it is a family's real ownership of a business that is often discussed as a competitive advantage of tenacious family businesses, with their long-term perspective (Ward, 1987).

One study of companies with stock ownership plans done for the Commerce Department found a statistical correlation between employee ownership and profitability. Other things being equal, the greater the equity the employees own, the greater the company's degree of profitability (Conte and Tannenbaum, 1978).

Human Resource Policies and Practices. Other than by equity, there are a variety of ways of increasing psychological ownership and commitment to growth among employees. Human resource policies that are caring, recognize individual differences, and promote respect and dignity, coupled with management that supports its people with the right tools (raw materials and information), promote high involvement and behavior that resembles that of proprietors. Some of the innovations in manufacturing organizations over the last twenty years are evidence of this (Poza, 1980, 1985). Gain-sharing and profit-sharing bonus plans that financially reinforce a "we are in this together" attitude also help create a sense of commitment that resembles that of equity ownership (Lawler, 1981).

The Politics of Survival for Interpreneurs

The founder of Allen, Miller and Partners, discussed earlier, recently transformed the company into an employee-owned organization as it moved into the hands of the second generation, in order to preserve high quality in designs and services beyond the first generation. A high-commitment, peer-based professional organization is his legacy to the next generation. His son has been an active codesigner of the entire transformation and regeneration of the business.

Today this company relies for its creative tasks on project teams led by team leaders. The overall management of the business depends on weekly management team meetings and a series of management committees: finance, personnel, and marketing. These in turn report to the member group, as the management team is called. A board of directors, with two outsiders sitting on it, meets twice a year to review the financial performance of the firm, provide management advice, review the annual budget and financial goals of the corporation, and monitor the firm's strategic direction.

One way interpreneurs have achieved major breakthroughs is by starting small, with broad goals, proceeding slowly and experimentally, and shying away from the spotlight in the early stages. There are good reasons for this pattern of success.

Politicians and strategic managers know that the way to avoid fueling the fires of early resistance to change is to keep the vision broad enough. This prevents polarization of others around the details of the idea, encourages those who join to further elaborate and shape the details, and allows room for mistakes. With time, enough adherents and objective results start showing up that the new idea can withstand the opposition.

Interpreneurs and their advisers need to keep the new idea or new venture simple and small. They need to conceive of it as a series of successive approximations to the intrepreneur's total vision; clearly define, bound, and structure the new-venture unit; and keep it separate from the rest of the company, preferably as a small team of peers in a simple, inexpensive setting (the classic garage, basement, or trailer).

Interpreneurs should dare to venture only on the basis of need and make sure that others see the need for higher profit margins or share the quest or obsession. An "angel" for the venture helps. Venture capitalists have long recognized that both money and sponsorship are key. Firms should also keep commitments flexible or negotiate agreements that prevent undue pressure for early positive results.

S. C. Johnson and Son is now stimulating growth after years of lethargy. This $2 billion consumer products giant, best known for its Johnson Wax line of products, is being run by a fifty-nine-year-old member of the fourth generation: Samuel C. Johnson, chairman and chief executive officer. Johnson is currently stimulating growth through a series of new policies, structures, and practices, all designed to promote interpreneurship by the fifth generation. Within the last several years, Samuel C. Johnson has instituted a matrix organizational structure to promote interdepartmental cooperation between functions (manufacturing, marketing, and so on). He has also created four business teams: personal care, home care, specialty chemicals, and insecticides. His purpose there is to promote responsibility and other behaviors akin to those of owners and reduce bureaucratic layers of management.

The Johnson Wax division has overhauled the compensation system to promote pay for performance, a concept quite alien to this traditionally paternalistic company. It has also increased the R & D budget significantly to improve knowledge of technology, and hired a new chief scientific officer. Finally, Samuel C. Johnson recruited and hired his son S. Curtis Johnson III to head a venture-capital unit that is investing in both related and unrelated businesses.

All this change making to facilitate interpreneuring comes out of a recognized need to support growth and innovation at a critical juncture for the company. Samuel C. Johnson's father had recognized a similar need a generation ago when he backed his son's idea for a new business unit—the Raid line of insecticides—which is currently one of the company's most profitable product lines.

This recommitment to growth and interpreneurship appears well timed for both the business and the family. In the late 1970s, as a result of diversifying too far afield from what Johnson managers knew best—personal and home care products—the firm suffered financial losses from a string of acquisitions in the leisure and recreational equipment business. Recoiling from this and several other market blunders, S. C. Johnson and Son headed for protected waters—core businesses where it had technical and marketing expertise—only to find more aggressive competition now feeding in those waters. Lethargy resulted in uncompetitive production costs and higher prices on the shelves, which led to eroding profit margins and loss of market share.

In the family front, we find the fifth generation having gone through college and now ready to make a contribution, though wondering what context to make it in. But with Samuel C. in his fifties and S. Curtis and other members of the fifth generation in their late twenties and early thirties, the probabilities of enlisting the next generation for continued interpreneurship are, psychologically speaking, the best they will ever be (Davis, 1982).

Time will judge the effectiveness of this case of interpreneurship, yet many of the essential elements are present: (1) changes in organization that promote greater autonomy and free-market dynamics, including the use of business teams; (2) changes in reward systems; (3) additions to the company's knowledge of technology and markets; (4) new information systems; and (5) a venture-capital unit led by an entrepreneur at heart, S. Curtis Johnson. The entrepreneurial fifth-generation Johnson often admits to liking the freedom to explore opportunities built into his job. And this ability to explore and commit, with passion, to new opportunities is at the heart of interpreneurship and continued growth.

Summary

Strategic exploration and planning by family and firm, organizational change and development, financial restructuring, stock ownership, and behavioral changes in the family system all set the stage for interpreneurship and continued growth. Task or business teams, changes in reward and information systems, diversification or specialization primarily in areas where technology and market knowledge already exists, and in-house entrepreneurial approximations are interventions that support interpreneurship and continued business growth. While extensive evidence is lacking, the comprehensive and consistent use of several of these interventions appears to be optimal to stimulating interpreneurship.

The choice of interpreneuring practices will have to be sensitive to the business's and the family's cultures as well as to the firm's technical and marketing expertise.

Many entrepreneurs and interpreneurial families, particularly those involved in highly successful businesses, have so much of their identity and social status defined by the original product, service, or market served that choosing to expand in new directions creates extreme tension and discomfort. Much more than money is at stake.

The appropriateness of the choice will also depend on the degree to which interpreneurial structures, policies, and practices have previously been used at the firm, on the financial status of the firm, and on general economic conditions. Interpreneuring is most likely to succeed when:

1. The business possesses a culture that is well suited to the ambiguity and risk taking of entrepreneurial activity as evidenced by the organization's history.
2. Management supports the new venture with structures, policies, and practices that separate the young venture from the old businesses and shelter it from corporate burdens (such as high overheads) that it cannot carry.
3. A long-term investment perspective exists regarding financial resources committed to the new venture. Young entrepreneurs have no use for "nervous money."
4. The family culture of the family in business supports such new ventures.

11

How to Achieve
Smart Business Growth

Although it is not easy to summarize fifteen years of consulting experience, I attempt to do so in this chapter, to promote informed and concerted action while the ideas covered in the book are still fresh in your mind.

Again and again, I have found ten characteristics in evidence in businesses ready to undertake the arduous task of smart growth. I list and discuss them here to enable you to assess how much readiness to pursue growth exists among owners and business associates in your company—and discover ways to stimulate the development of these ten qualities where they are lacking.

Similarly, several tactics are used more consistently and frequently than others for revitalization and smart growth among businesses at the crossroads. These, too, I list and discuss here, as the initial impetus to get the firm started in its growing efforts.

Because CEOs and next-generation leaders are crucial in planning smart growth, I have written special letters to these readers that should provide each of the two groups of leaders both with new perspectives on working together to stimulate business growth and with encouragement to take the first few steps in that direction. If you are interested in reading the story of an exceptional company that is once again in the phase of regeneration and smart growth, I also encourage you to read Resource B, following this chapter.

Ten Characteristics of Businesses Ready to Grow

Any business that is to successfully negotiate the crossroads and achieve growth must possess ten essential characteristics:

1. The business perceives an inevitability to growth, perhaps due to the high risk of decline (even potential total loss of the company) unless growth is promoted, or perhaps due to the overwhelming attractiveness of a particular growth option—one that perfectly matches the company's strengths and the family's circumstances.

2. The nature of the business is defined narrowly, by niches in which the business's competitive strengths lie. At the same time, the business is defined broadly enough to allow serious consideration of product line extensions, geographical expansions, and/or diversification within familiar technology or markets or both.

3. Management is striving for better product quality, better customer service, and/or greater competitive fitness. A low-cost emphasis predominates throughout the company. Even if quality, technical innovation, or customer service, not selling price, are the key competitive determinants for the business, a long-term value-for-money orientation maintains the loyalty of customers.

4. There is clarity of and widespread agreement on company and family mission, vision, strategy, and growth plans. A strategic consensus helps ensure that financial and operating decisions are congruent with the growth direction of the business.

5. The firm's commitment to people associated with the business, be they family members, customers, or employees, is maintained through boom times and recessions. The evidence of this commitment is R & D and advertising budgets that are maintained at their usual levels during recessions, and associates and employees who are allowed to work through difficult times instead of being laid off.

6. The founder or CEO is interested in leaving a legacy, is committed to the next generation, and is willing to transfer power to the successor in a timely fashion. Life cycle experts suggest that a window of opportunity for succession exists during the CEO's mid fifties to mid sixties. Timely disengagement of the CEO allows the company's life to extend beyond his or her lifetime.

The founder's or CEO's withdrawal is managed and includes (1) a public statement of the CEO's changing role (which may include some continued involvement as, for example, consultant or board chairperson but with no operating or day-to-day responsibilities) by a certain date, (2) the CEO's or founder's commitment, through action, to an orderly succession (such action may include the formation of a task force, the sponsoring of retreats, or a published timetable of succession/transition events), and (3) active teaching and coaching of the next generation by the founder or CEO and direct involvement in making explicit the principles, philosophies, and strategies that underlie the business's past success.

7. A capital corporation structure or other owner-manager ownership mechanism exists and the estate plan is current, enabling both concentration of controlling ownership in the hands of managing/operating owners and equitable wealth distribution among family members who choose not to run the business.

8. The growth opportunity chosen simultaneously satisfies the needs and aspirations of family members and the competitive reality and strategy of the business. Only a good match for both systems enables solid long-term growth. The particular circumstances of the business and the family are at the heart of a well-conceived growth strategy. Unfortunately, the owner's own circumstances are also the ones that conspire against needed change and regeneration. That is a major dilemma, and it is one that competent outsiders can be invaluable in helping to manage. Another key task is the selection of a successor and his or her installment in the power of leadership. This is a key task in regenerating the business and the family, and in perpetuating them both.

9. Skills to manage the turbulence of the regeneration state exist in the business and in the family. Leadership understands the concepts and methods of systematically restructuring the organization to match the new growth strategy in a congruent fashion (as discussed in Chapter Ten); failing that, educational and consulting resources are sought to bring that knowledge in-house.

10. Social and business innovations that promote interpreneuring—that is, maintain the entrepreneurial edge across generations of owners and managers—are experimented with, imple-

mented, and adapted. Examples of these are active boards of directors, asset boards, steering committees, boards of advisers, and business teams. Such innovations are all attempts at exposing the organization further to its environment and subjecting it to the creative dynamics of free markets. In using these, innovative managers and owners turn threats into opportunities for competitive advantage, and weaknesses into internal challenges for adaptation and growth of the business and the family.

A Personal Call to Action

Only action that supports the unique growth strategy developed for your business (and owning family) will deliver the enterprise from the forces of decline present at the crossroads. Current CEOs and next-generation leaders are the primary shapers of such strategy and the primary decision makers for such action. The two letters that follow contain my message to the leaders of both generations.

A Letter to the CEO

The most important contribution you can make to family-business regeneration is to communicate widely your commitment to business continuity. The most important gift you can make to a family that is involved in management or ownership is to pass on your dream about the business—its legacy and future—and then allow each family member to make his or her choice about the nature of their involvement in the business.

You may not be the "retiring kind." After years of entrepreneurial activity, you may see working as the only way to have fun and maintain your self-esteem. But because you cannot take the business with you, you owe it to your aspirations of leaving a legacy, and to others who have grown to depend on you, to plan for the next generation's succession. Talk to your spouse about this; plan subsequent steps together.

Single-generation businesses are built on a different set of assumptions than cross-generational businesses: (1) that the business is just the source of a life-style, (2) that the business or its assets can be sold and the cash generated put to some other use, (3) that the business is not the legacy the founder or current CEO wants to leave (or perhaps he or she has no interest in leaving *any* legacy), (4) that nonfamily management can do a better job than next-generation family members of managing the business, and (5) that the family is not interested in the business. If these assumptions are true in your own circumstances, then communicate your intentions to keep the business to a single generation and let someone else be the architect for the next generation.

But if these five assumptions are not true in your case, there is no escaping your responsibility to carry out an orderly transition of power in the business. That means you have to choose a successor and vest in him or her your power *in your lifetime.* It means you have to help in the education of your successor, and you have to give this person the tools to lead: controlling ownership, an opportunity to be entrepreneurial and take risks (as you did in starting the business), and an active board of directors (one with two or three outsiders in it to broaden the dream, bring new ideas, and provide objective review of the management of the business).

While you carry out your succession actions, you may want to continue as senior researcher, consultant, or business diplomat. After all, you embody the company's image and reputation in the world, and it is time to harvest this goodwill for the sake of business continuity. But whenever you disagree with what you see being done by the next geenration during this period, do not forget that this new generation has grown up in today's world and may be far more attuned to the realities of doing business today than you are.

If, on the other hand, the business has become boring, by all means harvest some of your crops and do something that is more fun and revitalizing. If the next generation is not ready yet, build a bridge with nonfamily management. But do not let potential successors see you grow bored at the helm, or they will never join you in the business.

Handle your relationships with the next generation with care and love. Do not lose sight of the fact that while they were growing up, you or your spouse assumed the responsibility for managing these relationships. Adults that they now are, they may still expect you to take the lead on things having to do with getting along. So lead! Reach out! Communicate! Make time for these all-important responsibilities.

Help the next generation arrive at its own vision, and promote their use of competent consultants and advisers, even if you never had much use for them. A renaissance is a time of beauty, of vitality, of new beginnings. There is simply no better way for your business tenure to end.

A Letter to the Next Generation

The future of the enterprise belongs to you. The ownership of the future constitutes a responsibility way before it yields any authority or confers any benefits or perks on you. You are the agent of change and regeneration for the business, and this responsibility is likely to make your relationship with the previous generation a difficult one.

The burden for managing this relationship does not fall exclusively on the founder or earlier generation, though you might assume that it does. Although the responsibility for managing the relationship between parents and children is certainly the parents' throughout the years of childhood and early adulthood, this pattern often persists beyond the timeframe within which it is appropriate. Now you share the responsibility for managing the relationship with your boss (and your parent). And because parents and bosses are only human, their wisdom and maturity may not serve them as well on some occasions as you might have liked. The fact is that, the differences in age, experience, and authority in the business and family hierarchy notwithstanding, your relationship to your boss/parent is one of mutual dependence or interdependence.

Do not underestimate your dependence on your parent/boss for information, education, influence, and leadership capability in both the family and the business. But neither should you fail to recognize your parent's/boss's need to count on your loyalty, abilities, and commitment to regenerate the business. Regardless of your personal preferences and the life cycle dynamics between you and your predecessors, the business needs complementarity and full utilization of both generations' skills and abilities. Managing the dilemmas of this mutual dependency is an important task for you.

There is no better way to start than by overcommunicating. So many assumptions exist in long-standing relationships between people that new information needs to be generated through conversations that make explicit both parties' feelings, motivations, goals, strengths and weaknesses, reactions to pressure, work-style preferences, and concerns. The better the two of you know yourselves, of course, the higher the probability that these conversations will be fruitful. Without self-knowledge, both sender and receiver of information may significantly screen the content of the conversation without even realizing it. Therapeutic help for personal growth purposes may be something you want to consider, to help you know yourself better and screen less of your predecessor's communication.

Make sure that you work at maintaining a relationship that matches both generations' needs and work styles, one that acknowledges both the familial and business roles but differentiates between these two. The relationship also needs to be based on explicit expectations of each other and plenty of communication that acknowledges progress or lack of progress in meeting these.

Respect and honor the history of the business and your predecessor's role in it. Learn all you can about managing change, because unlike your predecessor, you are not starting from scratch; your entrepreneurial activity will be done in the context of all the growth that has preceded you. And do not forget the family. Its interests need to be considered as you make choices for the business. How you choose to lead and involve family members will have significant bearing on your ability to be successful in the business.

Key Tactics for Smart Growth

What I have learned in my years of consulting with entrepreneurial and family-owned businesses, sharing the thrill of victories and the agony of defeats in the battle for regeneration, can be captured in these few suggestions.

Schedule a major "wake-up call" for the business every

twenty to twenty-five years. One way to stem the tide of waste and broken dreams across generations is to avoid decline by revitalizing or regenerating the business every twenty to twenty-five years. To allow growth in the interim, management should define the nature of the business neither too narrowly nor too broadly. A lot of growth traditionally takes place at the boundaries of the original business concept. This kind of growth, close to home, builds on experience and expertise and thus allows the business to grow from strength rather than through diversification far afield.

As the regeneration starts to bear fruit, management, family, and employees should celebrate the victory. Success should never be allowed to blunt competitive ability by reducing a sensitivity to mistakes, problems, and bad news, however. Success needs to be celebrated, but then the next batch of challenges needs to be confronted head on—without ignorance, or worse yet denial, of the facts. It is hard to do, but information systems can help.

Challenge the organization: use information to influence and motivate. The competitive and entrepreneurial edge of a young firm is maintained only by the continuing challenges posed to the organization by its leaders. The growing firm would do well to invest in a sophisticated information system and keep cost figures and information on quality and customer service forefront in every employee's and owner's mind. I also recommend that firms form task teams and trouble-shooting committees, listen to their suggestions for improvement, and implement at least some of their recommendations. Management should never hesitate to bring in the bad news, to expose the organization to what others, including the competition, are doing. And never should leadership stop learning.

Commit to leaving a legacy and get consensus on a mission and vision for the business. Businesses do not have to die; CEOs do. But a legacy can live on. A legacy's vitality is dependent on how widely shared the commitment to the enterprise is among the next generation of owners/managers. Having widespread agreement on what business the company is in, what it stands for, and what strategic objectives it is pursuing also aids in avoiding misallocation of resources, loss of managerial energy, and conflictual relationships between people in the business and in the owning family. Involving people in discussions of mission, vision, strategy, and objectives is necessary. As consensus develops on a variety of issues along the way, it will be easier to develop consensus on major issues at times of crisis or periods of regeneration. For example, reinvestment of earnings in the business to promote growth and continued health may sometimes preclude or reduce dividends. Only if there are attractive larger, superordinate objectives will individual agendas or micro-objectives become less prominent. Growth and regeneration require collective energies and significant financial resources and thus depend on widely shared macro-objectives captured in vision, mission, and strategy statements.

Maintain a commitment to people. Customers and employees deserve the family firm's commitment through the thick and thin of business cycles. (Private companies have an easier time doing this—as Levi-Strauss found, having gone public and then private again under the leadership of the Haas family.) Far too many family-controlled businesses forget this people priority after the founding generation passes away.

Be leery of quick fixes and cosmetic improvements. Revamping the corporate logo, building new offices, or changing the packaging or appearance of the product is sometimes useful. When such steps assume priority status during times of crisis or rapid change, however, more often than not they are an excuse for not dealing with the real problems of the firm. Changing the image of the *Saturday Evening Post* was a priority of Curtis Publishing back in the 1960s, yet that goal paled in comparison to the need to change strategic direction.

Changing strategic direction can be confusing and difficult for family and employees, so managing the regeneration actively is a must. Time-sequenced activity plans, periodic communication meetings of the family and of employee groups, the selection and use of natural leaders as managers of specific change projects, and perhaps even the creation of a transitional organizational structure may be appropriate. Otherwise, the day-to-day business may not allow management the time to bring about the changes and regeneration needed.

Special skills are needed both in the firm and in the family to manage the regeneration state. Problem-solving, team-building, change-management, project-management, and leadership skills are all essential. But even more important than possession of the skills is their *use*. Managing the regeneration requires, above all, courage and the conviction that comes from serious commitment to the vision of growth by both management and family members.

RESOURCE A

Financing the Costs
of Growing a Business

Growth, as committed to first in your vision and then in your strategy and action plans, requires capital. The financing of new growth should be responsive to this vision, strategy, and action plans. Meshing your capital-raising strategies with your overall business strategy is the subject of this chapter.

The unique requirements of your business should not be a deterrent to the acquisition of capital for growth. Through my consulting work with growing companies and discussions with bankers, venture capitalists, and private investors, I have seen a broad spectrum of financial techniques. These have been varied enough to convince me that creative approaches to financing new growth are available to all firms, regardless of differences in financial and competitive situations.

Entrepreneurs generally experience significant tension in the process of availing themselves of other people's money to fund growth. Unless the commitment to growth is quite important to the long-term well-being of the business, many entrepreneurs choose not to dilute their control of the firm by allowing outsiders ownership in the business. Whether outsiders become involved through

Note: I would like to thank Michale Murphy, research assistant, and John B. Naylor, president of National City Venture Corporation, for their help in the preparation of this chapter.

175

loans (and some of their covenants), equity (and some of its holder's emphasis on short-term earnings), limited partnerships, joint ventures, or licenses and franchises, the interests of these new stakeholders certainly complicate the demands placed on a business leader.

Why borrow? Why go public? Why license your technology or franchise your marketplace? The answer lies in your own assessment of how appropriate are different rates of growth for your business, your family perhaps, and yourself. Your own preferences for pace—and your family's, in a family business—are important considerations. Your own abilities and those of your management team and involved family members are also key factors.

Ease of entry into your market is another important factor. The last thing you want to see happen, if you and your associates are committed to growth in a high-growth and high-profitability market niche, is to have the *Wall Street Journal* publish an article about you or your industry. But if it does, your strategy of slowly and quietly growing out of retained earnings would become questionable indeed. The opportunity for growth might elude your slow-growth firm and be taken by others more prone to aggressively financing new growth in your market niche.

The extent of your growth aspirations, as captured in your growth vision, is also a determining factor. You may recall from the discussion on deciding to maintain the business (in Chapter Two) that slow-growth aspirations have enabled some businesses to remain viable, without growth capital, for a few generations.

There are also many successful firms that have stimulated business growth but financed it internally, out of cash flows and retained earnings. White Castle, for example, now in its third generation of family management, has almost no debt on its balance sheet. Most unique in its industry, it has no franchisees, either. The approximately 220 restaurants it owns represent internally financed growth since the firm's birth in 1921. This self-reliance served it well during the Depression, when many others who had aggressively borrowed went broke. Could the founder and the second generation have sought external financing and grown faster? Could faster growth have preempted the proliferation of competing

McDonald's, Wendy's, and Burger Kings and made White Castle a larger factor in the fast-food business than it is today?

Finding appropriate ways of financing new growth is key to maintaining your business's entrepreneurial edge beyond the creation/birth stage. Interpreneurship—entrepreneurial action across generations—relies on money earmarked for growth, whether it is obtained through the sale of equity or through venture-capital firms, joint ventures with larger firms, limited partnerships with individual investors, more traditional debt and government financing, or even financing from positive cash flow.

Each of these financing categories will be explored thoroughly in the pages that follow. This discussion should help you, the chief executive officer or owner-manager, decide which growth-financing approach is more appropriate to your unique situation. It should also help promote discussions with your chief financial officer, your family (if family members are in the business), and your board of directors (if you have one) about meshing financing strategy with the overall business strategy.

Going Public

Issuing and selling company stock raises permanent capital for growth. Because this money does not have to be repaid, the financial condition of the company improves immediately when management takes this step. Going public does not in any way hamper additional efforts to obtain financing, as debt would, and does not subject your business to the shifting winds of interest rates, company sales, and growth of the economy. Money derived from the sale of stock does not raise your business's break-even point, as interest payments would. In cost-competitive market niches, this benefit is a worthwhile consideration.

If the stock price increases after the offering, a strong after-market may develop for the shares. This would enable you to obtain future financing at even more favorable terms than the initial offering. This strong "public" image would enhance any of your other efforts at obtaining favorable financing for growth, whether through debt or through joint ventures or combinations with other businesses. A highly valued publicly traded stock would enable your business to acquire other firms in tax-free exchanges of stock and would allow you to secure loans with the stock as collateral.

If you provide a market value for your stock, both your own and your family's financial condition would be more liquid and flexible. Diversification of the estate would be made possible without forcing the business to diversify into markets or technologies it knows little about. Conglomerates, large or small, are less easily managed and less profitable than companies that remain focused on what they do best (Porter, 1980).

Companies whose shares are publicly traded also enjoy a degree of visibility and recognition that you may want for your business. Public recognition of what you have created and the legacy it promotes have value. (On the other hand, you may prefer privacy and obscurity, and the competitive advantages these give you.) If you are entertaining the kind of accelerated growth that requires ownerlike commitment from your employees, employee stock incentive plans are more attractive if the shares are public. This gives them liquidity, makes them exchangeable for cash.

But accepting equity capital is accepting an outsider's permanent claim on your firm's future earnings and diluting ownership of your business. It means loss of privacy and a limiting of owners' and managers' freedom to act; analysts, a board of directors, and shareholders may all review actions taken. Some of these reviews may be biased in the direction of short-term considerations—earnings, dividends, stock price today—and sacrifice the long-term vision of the owners.

Going public is costly. Fees from underwiters, accountants, and attorneys can exceed 10 percent of the total offering price. And in a market where raiders are heroes, control could be taken from the owners in fairly short order; what took a lifetime to build could be promptly dismembered. Measures exist to control this risk, of course. The offering could include voting and nonvoting common stock, for example. This could keep owners in control even if they held less than 50 percent of the common.

If you decide to go public, timing is important. What are your other personal commitments? How are the equity markets doing? Is your particular industry in or out of favor right now? Does your company have strong earnings momentum at this time?

The number of companies having successful initial public offerings varies considerably from year to year, as does the price-earnings ratio at which the market is willing to buy the shares. You want to sell at the higher end of the range.

Remember, you are selling shares in order to get money— money that you intend to use in stimulating business growth. But the time when you need it may not be the best time to get it via a public offering. (If you are interested in reading further on the mechanics of public offerings and its reporting requirements, consult *The Arthur Young Guide to Financing for Growth,* by Owen, Garner, and Bunder, 1986.)

Nothing will ever be quite the same after you go public. Every facet of your business's character and operations will feel the impact. Even the American Institute of Certified Public Accountants recognizes the importance of the owner's personal considerations and emotional needs in the decision (American Institute of Certified Public Accountants, 1982). And some research suggests that the most significant barriers to going public are indeed psychological (Dailey, Reuschling, and DeMong, 1977). After having worked so hard at birthing the baby, founder-entrepreneurs are not inclined to share the glory with others, nor are they receptive to the potential for interference by the SEC and strangers with different motivations about their investment.

Still, going public is the culmination of many owner-managers' ambitions for their growing business. Notice how the discussion hinges on your answer to a question discussed in Chapter Three: What is my vision for myself and the company? What does going public mean to you? Growth, freedom, flexibility, professionalization? Or does it mean selling out, giving up, even death of a sort?

Going public is a demanding process that can best be accomplished with the help of professionals—investment bankers, attorneys, and venture capitalists—especially if they have been involved with you previously. For the company intending to raise less than $7.5 million, there is some help available: an alternative to the time and expense of the SEC's standard S-1 registration of securities. The recently developed S-18 registration requires significantly less information and red tape. Given the difficulty and expense of the process, however, going public should still be limited to large capital requirements—say, $2 to $5 million or more.

But if you can accumulate some capital to grow by means other than going public, and if you can demonstrate strong sales and earnings growth as a result, your shares may be worth a lot more in the future. If that approach appeals to you, a private placement or more traditional debt financing may be in order for now.

Deciding on a Private Placement

The most private way to raise capital is from the original owner or owners. Bringing in a new partner or partners, for example, maintains your privacy and control while giving you growth capital. Silent partners (nonmanaging investors) may be especially attractive.

A private placement is the sale of stock in your company to a limited number of private investors. Because such investors are exempt from SEC registration requirements, this alternative is less costly to implement than going public. These offerings typically can raise a more limited amount of money than a public offering ($500,000 or less) but in a relatively shorter timeframe. They are also a lot more accessible to companies that still do not have the track record or reputaton that would sell a public offering.

Another advantage of a private placement is that it poses little threat to control of the company by outside investors. Such an offering, whether sold to those who are already interested in your firm (family and friends included) or to professional investors located by your broker, can bring the company a comparatively simpler injection of capital for growth.

Limited partnerships have also proven a very successful variation on the private placement theme, even after tax law changes effective in 1987 made their attractiveness from a tax standpoint disappear. Jones Intercable is a classic example of a firm that stimulated business growth via limited partnerships. Through several offerings starting in the early 1970s, this company has raised about $450 million from limited parters; Glenn Jones, owner, has used that capital to acquire cable TV systems in cities, suburbs, and rural areas all over the country. His typical partnership consists of $5,000 units. For that amount, investors received their initial investment back, plus 75 percent of a cable system's appreciation on sale and all the depreciation and tax advantages. Jones Intercable, with its related subsidiaries, is now the country's twelfth-largest cable TV operation (Block, 1986). Master limited partnerships can now also trade in stock exchanges as shares of stock, but without the double taxation (corporate and individual) and significant reporting requirements involved in public common stock.

Employee stock ownership plans are an attractive possibility under the private placement category. Tax laws provide incentives for ESOPs. Banks lending to companies restructuring under ESOPs get tax breaks that enable them to lend money at lower rates. With this money, borrowed at lower rates, employees buy shares in the business. The original owner achieves greater liquidity, and the company retains or increases the capital it has available for growth.

Private placement securities are restricted differently in their resale and transfer, depending on the nature of the filing your business chooses. The SEC's Regulations D and 4(6) apply and should be consulted. Again, there is no substitute for professional help in this area. Even though private placements are exempted from SEC registration requirements, your business could be liable for fraud or other allegations by private investors. Doing the placements correctly is essential to legally uncomplicated growth.

Financing Through Venture Capital

While the term *venture capital* sounds high-tech, this form of financing has its roots in family businesses, where fathers, brothers, or aunts were asked to venture or risk some money for the promise of high returns. Take American Research and Engineering, in Chicago, mentioned in Chapter Ten. It has set up its own trust to enable the next generations of family to engage in entrepreneurial activity. The founder recognized that the family business as created by one generation could be a poor fit for the next generation. The trust that he created for new ventures funds children in the family in their business ventures (after review of their proposals by a family board). Theirs is an in-house, in-family venture-capital firm.

Venture capitalists are at the leading edge of private investors. Venture-capital firms today expect annual returns anywhere from 25 to 50 percent, depending on risk perception and stage of business growth, to compensate for the higher risk in this type of investment. And unlike bankers, they tend to take a more hands-on approach to their investment in your company. They will analyze, recommend, and introduce you to potential customers and top-flight managers in your industry. Venture capitalists—whether working out of investment banking firms, as individual investors, or out of venture-capital firms—tend to concentrate in one or selected industries; thus their contacts and their advice on strategy, marketing, and finances can be as valuable as their money.

The venture-capital industry has grown significantly in the last several years. In 1986, 587 firms were registered as venture capitalists, a 148 percent increase in a decade. These firms raised approximately $4.5 billion in financing, a 36 percent increase over 1985's $3.3 billion. More of these firms are shifting their financing from seed money for high-technology projects to leveraged buy-outs and new business opportunities in businesses as mundane as office supplies retailing.

As more venture-capital firms are established and both federal and state governments decide to promote small businesses in different parts of the country, smaller firms will increasingly come into consideration by venture capitalists. Already the government, through Small Business Administration (SBA) loans to privately capitalized small-business investment companies (SBICs) and minority-enterprise small-business investment companies (MES-BICs), lends venture money to companies. (See Resource B for the case of Stew Leonard's Dairy, whose growth was partially financed by SBA loans.)

Most private venture-capitalist investments have financed new startups or a firm's research and development in a new area. But startup financing for a new product line by an established firm with a track record is increasingly available. Venture capitalists will take stock in the company (or holding company, in the case of a newly formed subsidiary), or may even agree to interest payments for the amount loaned, as in traditional debt financing. If stock is chosen, it is usually with the expectation of taking it public and realizing substantial profits in the sale.

Central to discussions with venture capitalists is the business plan. The results of your visioning and strategic planning have to be assembled into a growth plan that meshes your financial needs with your manufacturing, marketing, technical, and managerial capabilities. It should also include sales and income projections. The business plan is crucial, because negotiations with venture capitalists are very individualized; they proceed on a case-by-case basis.

Local business schools may be a good resource for help in finding venture capitalists in your area. Faculty members engaged in courses on business strategy and entrepreneurship have contacts or have developed their own investor network. John Aram and Kirk Neiswinder, for example, at Case Western Reserve University in Cleveland, Ohio, have developed a Great Lakes Region investor profile.

Venture capitalists may also be located by consulting the directory of the National Venture Capital Association, 1655 North Fort Meyer Drive, Suite 700, Arlington, VA 22209 or periodic listings appearing in *Inc.* and *Venture* magazines. The August 1989 issue of *Venture* carries a listing of "The Venture Capital 100," with addresses. These firms represent over 75 percent of the total financing done by the venture-capital industry. Another excellent guide is Arthur Lipper's Venture*'s Financing and Investing in Private Companies* (1988).

Entering into Joint Ventures

Joint ventures with larger companies that see you as their opportunity to enter a new and growing market can finance your growth. Joint ventures are often established as "trial marriages" and may lead to more permanent arrangements: mergers or acquisitions. That is why the structuring of the shared project needs to be carefully done, legally binding, and detailed in respect to endings or transition mechanisms. The joint venture can be incorporated separately or be structured as a limited partnership. Either way, your business would be capable of financing new growth with

objectives such as growth. Short-term funds are more available to smaller enterprises from bankers, who consider this a less risky way to lend money.

The risks of using short-term funds for long-term objectives are plentiful. The lender, no matter how well intentioned, may not be able to extend or reissue the loan. Administrative costs related to reissuing the debt add up. Short-term funds show up in your balance sheet as current liabilities and therefore hurt your financial status by lowering your current assets to current liabilities ratio; this often results in increased financing costs. More important, when the reasons for assuming a short-term loan are long-term in nature, the ever-present deadline makes business owners mind the bank more than the store.

Whether short- or long-term debt is used, then, should be determined by how your business will put the money to work. In either case, it is important to prepare properly to seek the funding. Having an up-to-date business plan and establishing good banking relationships way before seeking a loan are the basics.

In certain situations, short-term funds are the appropriate way to finance operations (and even certain kinds of growth). Short-term borrowing is appropriate when working capital is needed to finance inventory or receivables over the fluctuations in the business cycle, or to take advantage of some unusual and timely opportunity.

Like long-term loans, short-term borrowings can be secured or unsecured, depending on the lender's preference and your own creditworthiness in their eyes. Secured loans will involve the pledging of receivables or inventory. If receivables are pledged, they can be used as collateral or may actually be sold to a factor of their full value. Receivable financing is expensive, but it is no longer considered an indication of financial difficulties.

Inventory financing involves the pledging of inventory as security for the loan. Traditional financial institutions are conservative about the kind of inventory they will accept and the percentage of its value they will lend. Independent asset-based lenders are an expensive alternative. In exchange for higher interest rates (about six points over prime rate is common), they are willing to assume greater risks and may be worth considering as lenders of last resort (Mamis, 1987). Personally secured loans pose additional risks to you and should also constitute last-resort financing.

Commercial sources for long-term debt include a number of financial institutions. Term loans from commercial and investment banks are best known. In evaluating the benefits of such loans, you must consider that, while they do not dilute ownership, their terms and restrictions may have as great an impact on the owner's control as a sale of stock. In fact, investment banks, like venture capitalists, will often participate in debt financing only if going public or selling out is on the horizon. Underwriting fees is their bread and butter. On the other hand, much like venture capitalists, investment bankers come not just with money but with valuable advice and contacts. At the right time, these could be key to stimulating business growth.

Another institution to consider is the neighborhood savings and loan. Recent changes in banking law enable many of them to make commercial loans, and their local orientation can make them particularly receptive to the growth-financing needs of entrepreneurial and family businesses. Insurance companies, pension funds, and industrial associations (with their cooperative financing) are still additional sources of financing worth exploring. The costs of financing through them can be quite competitive.

Finally, the government should not be overlooked as a source of funds. The Small Business Administration makes few direct loans to businesses but guarantees many commercial loans that otherwise would not be extended by private lending institutions. Business and Industrial Development Corporations (BIDCOs) are a new class of state development finance vehicle. They are designed to meet the small firm's needs for moderate- to high-risk long-term debt and equity capital. They do this by also tapping the SBA loan guarantee program on 90 percent of the loaned amount.

Still another novel approach to carrying a guarantee is to assemble a well-regarded group as board of directors. If you or your family is well connected socially or professionally, having little money to grow the business is no excuse. Invite your notable friends to join you on the board of an exciting, growing venture and watch the bankers finance your growth plans.

Looking Internally for Capital

Like White Castle, Noxell relies primarily on its earnings and cash flow to fund rather aggressive growth. This is the very best way to raise capital. In 1987, Noxell had no outstanding debt. The company had revenues of approximately $700,000 in 1948. By 1966, fifty years after the company was founded by G. Lloyd Bunting, its sales had increased to over $38 million. By 1987, sales for Noxell— which besides Noxzema and Cover Girl brings us Lestoil and Wick Fowler's 2-Alarm Chili—had reached $489.5 million.

Noxell is very committed to growth, and has been throughout the three generations of Buntings. It has always earmarked money for new products, line extensions, modest acquisitions, and extensive advertising of their new and mature products. But that money has come from within the firm. Besides having no debt, the Bunting family still controls approximately 83 percent of Noxell voting stock.

Cost reduction, better cash management, and reinvestment of retained earnings in the business are the areas where internal funds for growth originate. Working capital financing is the foundation of well-financed growth efforts. It is ironic that these are the funds that corporate raiders first tap in their efforts to perform magic overnight in corporate capital structures. Can you tap this source of permanent financing for growth? Can you afford *not* to?

Commerce Clearing House, a publicly traded and family-controlled company, sits on cash reserves of about $75 million. It has amassed these funds for growth by a combination of going public (the family still holds 56 percent of the stock), retaining earnings rather than increasing dividends, and being quite careful about acquisitions. In fact, their commitment to quality sometimes yields only one possible use for retained earnings: repurchasing of company stock instead of acquiring for growth in size (Sherman, 1984).

While this is a more fortunate situation than most entrepreneurial and family-owned businesses find themselves in, nearly all growing businesses can improve their working capital and cash positions by better management of inventories, receivables, payables, and cash on hand. A look at a case involving one of my clients is a good illustration. To preserve anonymity, a fictitious name is used.

Unfortunately, Great Lakes Industries could not arrange to pay its raw material suppliers, personnel, lenders, and vendors when it got paid by its customers for the products that absorbed these costs. If it could have, cash-flow management would have been unnecessary. Great Lakes' situation is one all businesses are in. Only predominantly cash businesses, such as retailers or mail-order houses, have an easier time of it.

The time it took Great Lakes Industries' costs to be matched or covered by its sales receipts is what is often referred to as the cash-flow cycle. Managing this cash-flow cycle yielded significant permanent capital for growth in their case. Let us look at the cash-flow cycle components in Great Lakes' situation.

Before a CEO-led initiative on cash management, raw materials stood in a warehouse for an average of twenty-eight days before they were used by production. Then production averaged seventeen days to make finished product out of these; in other words, there was a seventeen-day work-in-process figure. Once production delivered product to the warehouse, it sat there for about thirty-three days of finished goods inventory before it was shipped and invoiced. Despite management's efforts at controlling inventories, the situation had recently worsened when a major customer implemented a just-in-time (JIT) program that forced Great Lakes to hold what would previously have been the customer's incoming materials inventory. Accounts receivable averaged forty-five days, and because the business's cash was held in several accounts, fifteen days' worth was held so that operations could continue without triggering insufficient funds situations. Because the owner-CEO was keen on maintaining a good reputation and relationship with suppliers, the policy was to pay in thirty-five days or less. Payables averaged thirty days.

Great Lakes had 108 days of sales (28 + 17 + 33 + 45 + 15 − 30 = 108) invested in working capital. A company that approximated $10 million in annual sales was therefore financing $2,958,904 for operations alone. If that sum—almost $3 million—were reduced by just a third, Great Lakes could put $1 million to work financing its growth plans.

In an impressive effort by the CEO, his chief financial officer, and the entire top-management team, Great Lakes managed to tap its own capital to finance growth. Aided by its major customer's expertise in JIT progams, it implemented its own just-in-time. This reduced raw materials inventory to twenty-one days and work-in-process inventory to fifteen days. A multidepartmental team worked on billing delays and brought accounts receivable down to an average of forty days. Cash accounts were consolidated, and cash on hand was reduced to five days. The CEO agreed with his financial officer to be less conservative on payables and extended their thirty days to a still commendable forty days.

Great Lakes had therefore reduced its cash-flow cycle by fifty-three days and its working capital requirements by almost half, to $1,506,849. Now the business was financing its working capital out of earnings. Had it needed to borrow instead, the interest expense (assuming a modest 12 percent, although venture capital would have been at 30 percent) would have been about $355,000 a year.

The elements of working capital are these: raw material, work-in-process, and finished goods inventories, accounts receivable, accounts payable, and cash. Managing these effectively allows your business to finance its growth internally. The process is akin to improving the yields in your manufacturing process by improving quality and reducing scrap. It costs you less to grow a business this way, and it makes a positive impression on lenders, venture capitalists, or investors, should you need them for further growth financing later.

Two other approaches to discovering working capital and freeing it up to work in your growth agenda are tax management (including the timing of income and deductions, avoiding the double taxation of income, and inventory valuations) and the use of leasing. Leasing is a great example of the matching principle discussed earlier in this chapter. When you lease, you are effectively borrowing to pay on assets just as you use them and depreciate them. Leasing frees up capital tied up in plant and equipment and may allow you to finance your growth out of internal funds. Selling plant or equipment you had previously purchased and leasing it back actually raises capital that you can use to expand. Whether leasing makes sense for your business depends on your own situation and should therefore be adopted only in consultation with professionals.

The Need for Consensus and Planning

Arriving at a consensus on the appropriateness of growing the business along qualitative or size dimensions is easy in entrepreneur-dominated businesses. Companies in their creation/birth or early growth stages face growth decisions in the context of survival and are guided single-handedly in these by the passion of the founder.

But in later stages—maturity and early decline—the growth consensus is missing. Family businesses, especially, experience a lot of conflict and/or paralysis over the issue of growth. Differences of opinion over the desirability of growth become emotionally charged when nonworking owners seem to prefer a steady stream of dividends to the risk inherent in growth. Siblings who have not worked through all of their early childhood rivalries may have now switched places in the hierarchy; younger sibling, the CEO, wants growth, but older sibling, the controller, thinks the business is large enough as it is.

The estate plan may have provided for equally shared ownership among three, four, or five owners; thus ownership may be widely dispersed now in the third or fourth generation. Parent-offspring conflicts may be at a peak, with parent unable to let go and acknowledge the prospect of death and offspring unwilling to continue to operate under the shadow. What is to be done? How can a family rationally deal with the growth agenda and its financial requirements?

If there is enough money to satisfy the conflicting needs and desires of the multiple stakeholders, the need for a tight, single-focus consensus disappears. As a result, the business can proceed with financing some growth plans. Nonmanaging owners can count on their steady stream of dividends and do or work at whatever they like. The Tabasco McIlhennys have a growth-financing consensus in their family right now precisely because of their recognition that without the additional earnings that growth will bring in the future, the family is likely to become conflictual.

The Curtis-Bok family, on the other hand, was unable to arrive at a focused consensus to save Curtis Publishing. Absentee and dispersed owners were unable to forge an alliance; instead, they aided in paralyzing the board of directors. And yet the owners all had rather taxing financial commitments—to the Curtis Institute of Music, the Philadelphia Symphony, and other organizations.

Concentration of ownership in a single managing owner helps a business realize its vision. S. C. Johnson and Son's fourth-generation CEO is convinced that the ability of the business to survive and grow through the next generation depends on one person—the owner-manager—making the tough decisions. This means that although Sam Johnson is willing to break up the company among the children, he will not equally divide the shares of S. C. Johnson and Son, the family-owned company. He is also willing to give majority, controlling ownership to a single fifth-generation Johnson interested in running the whole show if the others are not interested in managing the business.

Planning for the continuation of the firm and the continued financial viability of family members is also essential. Ideally, owners diversify family wealth without diversifying the family business into areas where it lacks market or technical expertise. Some alternative methods follow:

- The creation of real estate trusts.
- Preferred stock recapitalizations that allow the retiring generation to derive income from dividends and give the next generation future capital appreciation possibilities in the shares of common stock.
- Private annuities to transfer ownership across generations.
- Buy-sell agreements protected by life insurance policies.
- Limited partnerships with each member of the next generation operating as the general partner of his or her own business unit.
- Multiple corporations with a capital corporation at the helm.

When all the family assets are vested in one operating business, individual needs and desires of the next generation are constrained and the financial health of the operating business is then at risk. When all your eggs are in one basket, that basket needs to be watched very closely and with single-minded purpose. Because this is often unrealistic with one operating firm that belongs to a diverse family, the estate plan needs to concentrate ownership wherever it is going to be managed (it could be in multiple corporations) and provide diversification and financial liquidity for the family members whose calling is not in management.

A good example of smart growth that has also been adeptly financed is Stew Leonard's Dairy, discussed next, in Resource B.

RESOURCE B

An Example of
Smart Business Growth:
The Stew Leonard Case

Stew Leonard's is the world's largest dairy store. It also stocks a large assortment of groceries and household products, which would seem to put it in a category with supermarkets. The average size of grocery stores doing over $10 million in sales is approximately 22,000 square feet (Family Firm Institute, 1988). Stew Leonard's dairy and retail complex, by contrast, covers 110,000 square feet, about 37,000 square feet of which is occupied by the store itself. In contrast to more traditional supermarkets, which often stock as many as 15,000 items, Stew Leonard's stocks about 800. Its product lines include the traditional dairy products (produced right on site at the dairy), along with produce, juice, meat, fresh seafood, poultry, baked goods, soft drinks, snacks, and hot and cold salad bars. Aside from Stew Leonard's own dairy products, most goods sold there are bought directly from producers, so that there is no need to go through brokers or distributors.

Stew Leonard's emphasizes high quality and excellent customer service, but it is also constantly seeking to lower the costs of operations and of goods sold. The Leonard family is convinced that the additional quality and service, coupled with competitive pricing, is the right competitive formula, one that ensures that customers will be satisfied and will keep coming back.

Sales have increased from approximately $43 million in 1980 to over $100 million in 1988. (Very little of this increase is due to inflation, which has been moderate during this period.) While the average grocery store does approximately $400 worth of business per square foot, Stew Leonard's does over $3,000 per square foot. Inventory turnovers are way above the industry average, and selling prices remain about 10 percent below those for the competition (that is, other supermarkets and grocery stores within a five-mile radius).

The owning Leonard family plays an active role in the enterprise. Stew Leonard, Sr., now fifty-nine and chairman of the board, represents the third generation of Leonards in the business. His father, Charles, owned and operated the dairy farm and a milk home-delivery business started by *his* father in 1923.

Stew senior worked with his father in the dairy and on the milk delivery routes. When his father passed away in 1950, Stew and his oldest brother, Jim, formed a partnership and owned and operated the business until the early 1960s, when Jim left to pursue other interests. Stew senior then, convinced that the milk home-delivery market was dwindling, seized the opportunity to redirect and regenerate the business. With a loan from the Small Business Administration, he built a store next to the dairy. That was the beginning of the Stew Leonard's of today.

Members of the fourth generation now occupy key operating positions in the business. Stew junior, thirty-four, was named president in 1985. His younger brother Tom, thirty-two, is in charge of the Danbury Farmer's Market and is running a full store operation there (starting in 1989). Beth, their sister, and her husband operate Bethy's Bakery, a major profit center in the Norwalk store. Another brother runs the popcorn concession; and another sister heads the personnel function, known as Team Headquarters. Several in-laws hold vice-presidential jobs, and their children also work in the store in various capacities.

Why Stew Leonard's Is Such an Excellent Example of Smart Growth and Interpreneurship

The history of Stew Leonard's growth and regeneration provides an excellent illustration of nine of the ten characteristics of a business that is ready to grow—and that also is currently using many of the key tactics for smart growth. (See Chapter Eleven.)

At Stew Leonard's, growth is perceived as inevitable by each succeeding generation. It is almost as if without growth there would be no stability for the family and the business. (As the Leonards would say, Have you tried to stay balanced on a bicycle without moving forward?)

The history of the business also demonstrates a sharply focused business strategy based on a niche definition of the core business and a willingness to grow cautiously but solidly from this core business. As we have seen, in the 1960s the growth of the business was from dairy and milk home-delivery business to grocery store (which has now had twenty-six additions built). In the late 1980s growth was from one store location to two. The two stores represent a much broader product line while meeting performance requirements for turnover, profit margin, and customer satisfaction.

Stew Leonard's is continually searching for ways of improving quality and customer service that will differentiate the enterprise from a commodity business. At the same time, there is an unrelenting pursuit of lower costs through avoidance of middlemen and the use of technology in the dairy (where four people can manage the production of 2.5 million gallons of milk and thousands of units of yogurt, ice cream, butter, and other products a year). Other factors that contribute to lower costs are use of current information technology in the store that keeps track of inventories and trends in customer demographics and tastes, and human resource policies that require multiple-skill performance from all team members—and train them for it.

There is a powerful and widely shared vision of growth. And clarity and agreement exist among the third- and fourth-generation owners about the family mission, the company mission, and the business's strategy and growth plans. Performance standards are explicitly stated and fair and uniformly enforced (to such an extent that one of Stew Leonard's sons was fired for nonperformance and rehired only on a contractual assurance of high performance in the new job).

Stew Leonard's is committed to people—as customers, employees, and suppliers. Customers are always number one, and according to Rule #1 posted at the store entrance, always right. Rule #2, also sculpted in stone at the entrance, reminds employees that if the customer is ever wrong, they should go back and read Rule #1. Weekly focus group meetings and the implementation of the one hundred or so suggestions received daily from customers provide further evidence of this commitment. Employees are team members who are treated like extended family. They are well rewarded for a job well done with high salaries, much recognition, and ample training and development opportunities. Stew Leonard's is equally committed to its suppliers: it not only tries to educate them about customer preferences and taste changes, but where possible, it uses a single supplier for most of its business in a given product category.

Stew Leonard, Sr., is clearly committed both to leaving a legacy and to transferring power to his successor in his lifetime. He is currently consulting with an outside adviser about handling succession in the family business. Stew senior has stated his concern for business continuity as follows: "Immortality is important to me. I want this to continue to be preserved as a family business" (Family Firm Institute, 1988). He currently spends half his time away from the business in speaking engagements or leisure travel, forcing members of the next generation to empower themselves to run the business.

The growth opportunities chosen—new products and departments in the Norwalk store and geographic expansion to the new Danbury store—satisfy the ambitions and financial needs of the family and so far appear to be more than satisfying the competitive needs of the business.

Social and business innovation is ubiquitous at Stew Leonard's. When team members train in multiple skills, listen to customers and help with customer service, they gather new clues for potentially profitable product line expansions and new product/service combinations. Bethy's Bakery started within the Norwalk store as a small experiment with baked goods. Today it is one of the most profitable departments. The new Danbury store is an outgrowth of a modest experiment by Tom, who opened a small farmstand in Danbury in the late 1980s. At Stew Leonard's they seem to have discovered the equation for smart growth and continued entrepreneurial activity across generations of Leonards.

Only an ownership equity structure that would promote concentration of equity in the hands of the owner-operators of the next generation is missing from what is so far a business growth success story. The equity is still held jointly by Stew senior and his wife. But structural separation between the main business and its offshoots, with members of the present generation running separate departments and stores, bodes well for a principle of equity distribution that differentiates among members of the new generation.

As for the key tactics in force at Stew Leonard's, information is consistently used to challenge and motivate. Data on inventory turns are posted, as are the results of focus group meetings. Profit margins are closely watched. And when team members make visits to competitors, it is with the expectation that the team members will bring back at least one new idea that can be implemented at Stew Leonard's. This process promotes continuing improvement in a business that is already a high performer.

A businesswide wake-up call, last issued in the 1960s, has again been made, and the revitalization troops of the fourth generation are out working to regenerate the business once more with the new departments in the Norwalk store and the new store in Danbury.

I, for one, do not know what the future holds for this business and its owning family. But I cannot help feeling very encouraged by the prospects for Stew Leonard's: the interpreneurial capability of the new generation, their commitment to each other and the family, and the fun they are having in the business are all signs of increased chances for smart growth, business continuity, and prosperity.

References

"Ackerman Looks Beyond the Post." *Business Week,* Jan. 18, 1969, pp. 26-28.

Adizes, I. "Organizational Passages: Diagnosing and Treating Lifecycle Problems of Organizations." *Organizational Dynamics,* Summer 1979, pp. 3-23.

American Institute of Certified Public Accountants. "Assisting Small Business Clients in Obtaining Funds." In *Small Business Practice Aid No. 1.* New York: American Institute of Certified Public Accountants, 1982.

Andresky, J. "But I'm Just the Piano Player." *Forbes,* May 4, 1987, pp. 56-57.

Aram, J. D., and Cowen, S. "The Directors' Role in Planning: What Information Do They Need?" *Long Range Planning,* 1986, *19* (2), 117-124.

Barach, J. A. "Is There a Cure for the Paralyzed Family Board?" *Sloan Management Review,* Fall 1984, pp. 3-12.

Barnes, L., and Hershon, S. "Transferring Power in the Family Business." *Harvard Business Review,* July/Aug. 1976, pp. 84-93.

Beckhard, R. "The Confrontation Meeting." *Harvard Business Review,* Mar./Apr. 1967, pp. 149-155.

Beckhard, R., and Dyer, W. G. Jr. "SMR Forum: Managing Change in the Family Firm—Issues and Strategy. *Sloan Management Review,* 1983, *24* (3), 59-65.

Beckhard, R., and Harris, R. *Organizational Transitions: Managing Complex Change.* Reading, Mass.: Addison-Wesley, 1987.

Berenbein, R. E. "From Owner to Professional Management:

Problems in Transition." *Conference Board Report No. 851.* The Conference Board, New York, 1984.

Biggadike, H. R. "The Risky Business of Diversification." *Harvard Business Review,* May/June 1979, pp. 103–111.

Block, A. B. "The Poet King of Cable TV." *Forbes,* Dec. 1, 1986, pp. 48–52.

"Bok, Edward William." *Who's Who in America,* 1928–1929, p. 313.

"Bok, Mary Louise Curtis (Mrs. Edward Bok)." *Who's Who in America,* 1928–1929, p. 313.

Bok, E. W. "The Boy Who Began with Three Cents," *Atlantic Monthly,* Feb./Mar. 1923, pp. 152–160.

Brittain, J. W., and Freeman, J. "Entrepreneurship in the Semiconductor Industry." Paper presented at the Academy of Management meeting, Chicago, Aug. 1986.

Cameron, K., Whetten, D., and Kim, M. "Organizational Dysfunctions of Decline." *Academy of Management Journal,* 1987, *30* (1), 126–138.

Chakravarty, S. N. "The Vindication of Edwin Land." *Forbes,* May 4, 1987, pp. 83–84.

Clifford, D. K., and Cavanagh, R. E. *The Winning Performance: How American Midsize Companies Succeed.* Toronto: Bantam Books, 1985.

Cohn, T., and Lindberg, R. A. *Survival and Growth: Management Strategies for the Small Firm.* New York: American Management Association, 1974.

Conklin, M. "Rance Crain and the Family Bible." *Madison Avenue,* 1986, *28* (1), 19–27.

Conte, M., and Tannenbaum, A. "Employer-Owned Companies— Is the Difference Measurable?" *Monthly Labor Review,* July 1978, pp. 23–28.

Culligan, M. J. *The Curtis-Culligan Story.* New York: Crown Publishers, 1970.

"Curtis Considers Sale of *Status, Jack & Jill,* and *Holiday* Magazines." *Wall Street Journal,* Feb. 5, 1970, p. 7.

"Curtis Estate Appears to Have Won Control of Troubled Concern." *Wall Street Journal,* May 22, 1969, p. 9.

"Curtis Publishing Files a Statement with SEC on Plan to Recapitalize." *Wall Street Journal,* June 13, 1972, p. 9.

Dailey, R. C., Reuschling, T. E., and DeMong, R. F. "The Family Owned Business: Capital Funding." *American Journal of Small Business,* 1977, *2,* 30–39.

Danco, K. *From the Other Side of the Bed: A Woman Looks at Life in the Family Business.* Cleveland: Ohio University Press, 1981.

Danco, L. *Beyond Survival.* Cleveland: Center for Family Business, 1975.

Davis, J. "The Influence of Life Stage on Father-Son Work Relationships in the Family Firm." Unpublished doctoral dissertation, Graduate School of Business Administration, Harvard University, 1982.

Davis, P. "Realizing the Potential of the Family Business." *Organizational Dynamics,* 1983, *12* (1), 47–56.

Donnelly, J. F. "Participative Management at Work." *Harvard Business Review,* Jan./Feb. 1977, pp. 128–138.

Drucker, P. F. "The Discipline of Innovation." *Harvard Business Review,* May/June 1985a, pp. 67–72.

Drucker, P. F. *Innovation and Entrepreneurship.* New York: Harper & Row, 1985b.

Dyer, W. G. Jr. *Cultural Change in Family Firms: Anticipating and Managing Business and Family Transitions.* San Francisco: Jossey-Bass, 1986.

Evans, J. H., and Evans, F. C. "A Small Manufacturer's Success Story." *Management Accounting,* Aug. 1986, pp. 47–49.

Family Firm Institute. Proceedings of annual meeting, Boston, Oct. 1988.

Finley, L. "Can Your Small Company Acquire Resources as Favorably as the Large Company?" *American Journal of Small Business,* 1984, *9,* 19–25.

Fix, J. L. "A Bundle of Sticks." *Forbes,* Nov. 18, 1983, pp. 202–206.

Friedrich, O. *Decline and Fall.* New York: Harper & Row, 1970.

Gautschi, C. L., and Werner, M. E. "Planning and Organizing for Internal Growth Ventures." *Managerial Planning,* 1983, *32* (3), 21–42.

George, W. W. "Task Teams for Rapid Growth." *Harvard Business Review,* Mar./Apr. 1977, pp. 74–83.

Gluck, F. "Vision and Leadership." *Interfaces,* 1984, *14* (1), 10–18.

Goldwasser, T. *Family Pride.* New York: Dodd, Mead, 1986.

Hackman, R. "The Transition That Hasn't Happened." In J. R. Kimberly and R. E. Quinn (eds.), *New Futures: The Challenge of Transition Management.* Homewood, Ill.: Dow-Jones Irwin, 1986.

Hall, R. I. "A System Pathology of an Organization: The Rise and Fall of the Old *Saturday Evening Post." Administrative Science Quarterly,* 1976, *21* (6), 185-211.

Harrigan, K. *Strategic Flexibility: A Management Guide for Changing Times.* Lexington, Mass.: Heath, 1985.

Hershon, S. A. "The Problem of Management Succession in Family Businesses." Unpublished doctoral dissertation, Graduate School of Business Administration, Harvard University, 1975.

Hoffman, H. M., and Blakey, F. "Growing Concerns: You Can Negotiate with Venture Capitalists." *Harvard Business Review,* Mar./Apr. 1987, pp. 16-24.

Hollander, B. S. "Family-Owned Business as a System: A Case Study of the Interaction of Family, Task, and Marketplace Components." Unpublished doctoral dissertation, School of Education, University of Pittsburgh, 1983.

Hyatt, J. "Too Hot to Handle." *Inc.,* Mar. 1987, pp. 52-58.

Jacobs, S. L. "It's Often Hard in Family Firm to Let the Children Take Over." *Wall Street Journal,* Mar. 4, 1983, p. 33.

Jonovic, D. *The Second Generation Boss: A Successor's Guide to Becoming the Next Owner-Manager of a Successful Family Business.* Cleveland: Ohio University Press, 1982.

Kepner, E. "The Family and the Firm: A Coevolutionary Perspective." *Organizational Dynamics,* 1983, *12* (1), 57-70.

Kiefer, C., and Senge, P. "Metanoic Organizations." In J. Adams (ed.), *Transforming Work.* Alexandria, Va.: Miles River Press, 1984.

Kiefer, C., and Stroh, P. "A New Paradigm for Organizational Development." *Training and Development Journal,* 1983, *37* (4), 27-35.

Kollmorgen Corporation Annual Report, 1979.

Lansberg, I. "The Succession Conspiracy." *Family Business Review,* 1988, *1* (2), 119-143.

Lauenstein, M. C. "SMR Forum: Diversification—The Hidden

Explanation of Success." *Sloan Management Review*, 1985, *27* (1), 49–55.

Lawler, E. E. *Pay and Organization Development*. Reading, Mass.: Addison-Wesley, 1981.

Levinson, H. "Conflicts That Plague the Family Business." *Harvard Business Review*, Mar./Apr. 1971, pp. 90–98.

Lewin, K. "Forces Behind Food Habits and Forces of Change." *Bulletin of the National Research Council*. 1943, *108*, 35–65.

Liataud, J. "Entrepreneurship and the Family." *Loyola Business Review*, 1983, *4* (1), 9–12.

"The Limited's Unlimited Growth." *Discount Merchandiser*, 1986, *26* (3), 98–100.

Lindell, M. "Renewal Strategies in Large High Tech Companies: The European Approach." *Technovation*, 1986, *5*, 183–189.

Lipper, A. Venture's *Financing and Investing in Private Companies: A Guide to Understanding Entrepreneurs and Their Relationships with Investors, Lenders and Advisors*. Chicago: Probus Publishing, 1988.

MacMillan, I., Low, M. and Starr, J., "Survey of Corporate Renewal Strategies." Report by the Foundation for Continuing Education of the Steel Service Center Institute and the Sol C. Snider Entrepreneurial Center, Wharton School, University of Pennsylvania, Sept. 1988.

Mamis, R. A. "Lender of Last Resort." *Inc.*, May 1987, p. 149.

Manegold, J. G., and Arnold, J. L. "Growing Concerns: An Easier Way to Go Public." *Harvard Business Review*, Jan./Feb. 1986, pp. 28–30.

"Meeting the Capital Need of Small Businesses: The Case for BIDCOS." *Business*, Oct./Nov. 1984, pp. 56–57.

Mintzberg, H. "Crafting Strategy." *Harvard Business Review*, July/ Aug. 1987, pp. 66–75.

Mintzberg, H., and Waters, J. "Tracking Strategy in an Entrepreneurial Firm." *Academy of Management Journal*, 1982, *25* (3), 465–499.

Mintzberg, H., and Waters, J. "Of Strategies, Deliberate and Emergent." *Strategic Management Journal*, 1985, *6*, 257–262.

Morita, A. "When Sony Was an Up-and-Comer." *Forbes*, Oct. 6, 1986, pp. 98–102.

Murray, T. J. "The Perilous Pursuit of Sexy Businesses." *Dun's Business Month,* Nov. 1986, pp. 36–40.

Nelton, S. "Strategies for Family Firms." *Nation's Business,* June 1986, pp. 20–28.

Nelton, S. "Passing on the Dream." *Nation's Business,* Dec. 1987, pp. 55–58.

Norburn, D., Manning, K., and Birley, S. "Beyond Intrapreneurship: The Metamorphosis of Larger Corporations." *Leadership and Organizational Development Journal,* 1986, 7 (3), 21–26.

Owen, R. R., Garner, D. R., and Bunder, D. S. *The Arthur Young Guide to Financing for Growth.* New York: Wiley, 1986.

Parr, J. G. "Look Out McDonald's." *Forbes,* Dec. 30, 1985, p. 112.

Parr, J. G. "A Pair of Opposites." *Forbes,* Dec. 29, 1986, pp. 84–85.

Pascarella, P. "Meeting of the Minds." *Industry Week,* Oct. 17, 1983, pp. 59–60.

Pascarella, P. *The New Achievers.* New York: Free Press, 1984.

Peters, T., and Waterman, R. *In Search of Excellence: Lessons from America's Best Run Companies.* New York: Harper & Row, 1982.

Pinchot, G. *Intrapreneuring: Why You Don't Have to Leave the Corporation to Become an Entrepreneur.* New York: Harper & Row, 1985.

Pirsig, R. M. *Zen and the Art of Motorcycle Maintenance: An Inquiry into Values.* New York: Morrow, 1974.

Porter, M. *Competitive Strategy.* New York: Free Press, 1980.

Posner, B. G. "Mutual Benefits." *Inc.* June, 1984, pp. 82–92.

Posner, B. G. "The 100-Year-Old Start-Up." *Inc.* Oct. 1985, pp. 8–11.

Poza, E. "Managerial Practices That Support Interpreneurship and Continued Growth," *Family Business Review,* 1988, *1* (4), 339–359.

Poza, E. "A Do-It-Yourself Guide to Group Problem-Solving." *Personnel,* Mar./Apr. 1983a, pp. 69–77.

Poza, E. "Twelve Actions to Strong U.S. Factories." *Sloan Management Review,* 1983b, *25* (1), 27–38.

Poza, E. "Comprehensive Change-Making." *Training and Development Journal,* 1985, *39* (2), 81–85.

Poza, E., and Fuchs, C. "Improving Morale and Customer Service in Banks: A Case History." *Personnel,* May 1987, pp. 58–61.

Poza, E., and Marcus, M. L. "Success Story: The Team Approach to Work Restructuring." *Organizational Dynamics,* Winter 1980, pp. 2–25.

"Private Source for Long-Term Financing." *Small Business Report,* Apr. 1985, p. 98.

Prokesch, S. "Rediscovering Family Values." *New York Times,* June 10, 1986, p. D1.

Quinn, J. B. *Strategic Change: Logical Incrementalism.* Homewood, Ill.: Dow-Jones Irwin, 1980.

Quinn, J. B. "Managing Innovation: Controlled Chaos." *Harvard Business Review,* May/June 1985, pp. 73–84.

Rhodes, L. "New Management Pioneer, Jim Swiggett." *Inc.,* Feb. 1987, pp. 35–44.

Richman, T. "A Tale of Two Companies." *Inc.,* July 1984, pp. 37–43.

Roberts, E. "New Ventures for Corporate Growth." *Harvard Business Review,* July/Aug. 1980, pp. 134–142.

Roberts, E., and Berry, C. "Entering New Businesses: Selecting Strategies for Success." *Sloan Management Review,* 1985, *27* (2), 3–17.

Rose, J. T. "Interstate Banking and Small Business Finance: Implications from Available Evidence." *American Journal of Small Business,* 1986, *11,* 23–39.

Rumelt, R. P. "Diversification Strategy and Profitability." *Strategic Management Journal,* 1982, *3,* 359–369.

Sabel, C. F., Herrigel, G., Kazis, R., and Deeg, R. "How to Keep Mature Industries Innovative." *Technology Review,* Apr. 1987, pp. 27–35.

Schein, E. H. *Organizational Culture and Leadership: A Dynamic View.* San Francisco: Jossey-Bass, 1985.

Schumpeter, J. *Capitalism, Socialism and Democracy.* New York: Harper & Row, 1962.

Segal, M. "Changing Families and Changing Organizations: Applying Bowen's Theory." *Social Change,* Mar. 1986, p. 17.

Seneker, H. "How to Diversify and Like It." *Forbes,* Aug. 12, 1985, pp. 41–42.

Sherman, S. P. "The Company That Loves the U.S. Tax Code." *Fortune,* Nov. 26, 1984, pp. 58–64.

Shoeffler, S., Buzzell, R., and Heany, D. "Impact of Strategic Planning on Profit Performance." *Harvard Business Review,* Mar./Apr. 1974, p. 141.

Shuman, J. C., and Seeger, J. A. "The Theory and Practice of Strategic Management in Smaller Rapid Growth Firms." *American Journal of Small Business,* 1986, *11* (1), 7-18.

Stavro, B. "Now Comes the Hard Part." *Forbes,* Aug. 12, 1985, p. 58.

Stavro, B. "Some Lessons for the Big Boys." *Forbes,* Mar. 24, 1986, 138-140.

Stevenson, R. W. "How Anheuser Brews Its Winners." *New York Times,* Aug. 4, 1985, p. F1.

Sykes, H. B. "Lessons from a New Ventures Program." *Harvard Business Review,* May/June 1986, pp. 69-74.

"T & M's Seeds of Growth." *Marketing,* Nov. 13, 1986, pp. 33-35.

Trachtenberg, J. "Latin Beat." *Forbes,* Oct. 1, 1984. pp. 234-238.

"Trying to Bring Out the Old Shine at Johnson Wax." *Business Week,* Aug. 13, 1984, pp. 138-145.

Viscione, J. A. "Growing Concerns: How Long Should You Borrow Short?" *Harvard Business Review,* Mar./Apr. 1986, pp. 20-24.

von Hippel, E. "Users as Innovators." *Technology Review,* 1978, *8* (3), 31-39.

Ward, J. L. "Perpetuating the Family Business: Challenges Facing Siblings." *Loyola Business Forum,* 1986, *6,* 1-3.

Ward, J. L. *Keeping the Family Business Healthy: How to Plan for Continuing Growth, Profitability, and Family Leadership.* San Francisco: Jossey-Bass, 1987.

Ward, J. L. "The Special Role of Strategic Planning for Family Businesses." *Family Business Review,* 1988, *1* (2), 105-117.

Weiss, L. A. "Start-Up Businesses: A Comparison of Performance." *Sloan Management Review,* 1981, *23* (4), 37-53.

Index